105 MEADOWLARK READER

A Kansas Journal of Creative Nonfiction

ISSN: 2767-5254

D0873345

Quincy Press

Meadowlark Press
— since 2014 —

meadowlark-books.com

Editor, Cheryl Unruh
Quincy Press, www.quincypress.com

Published by
Meadowlark Press, LLC, meadowlark-books.com
PO Box 333, Emporia, KS 66801, USA
All rights reserved.

First Run Printed by: POD Print, Wichita, Kansas, podprint.com

Cover Photo by Scott Branine
flickr.com/photos/scott_branine/

CATALOGING DATA:
105 Meadowlark Reader / Bicycles / Issue 3: Spring 2022 /
[edited by] Cheryl Unruh [and] Tracy Million Simmons /

LITERARY COLLECTIONS / Essays
BIOGRAPHY & AUTOBIOGRAPHY / Personal Memoirs

Issue 3: Spring 2022—"Bicycles"
ISBN: 978-1-956578-15-7
ISSN: 2767-5254

Lifecycle

tonight's Moment of Zen
was brought to me by
some first-bloom, black-eyed Susans
blue-hue soybean fields
a sinking orb ablaze to the sound
of Gordon Lightfoot's "Sundown"
and exceeding the speed limit
on my engineless two wheels
on my fastest ten-mile loop of summer

—Rebekka Rohrback

105 Meadowlark Reader is a real paper
publication committed to including stories
from every Kansas county.

—32 stories from 37 counties in issue #3—

Our Reader features:

- True stories we hope will remind you of the deeply
  embedded Kansas roots we share.

- Funny stories. Heartfelt stories.

- Stories that may surprise you.

- Stories that may inspire you to contribute your own to
  future issues of *105 Meadowlark Reader.*

Contents

105 Supporters

105 MEADOWLARK READER

A Kansas Journal of Creative Nonfiction

Issue #3: Spring 2022

Bicycles

Dear 105 Reader,

Strap on your helmet, grab your handlebars, and ride along on these thirty-two incredible bicycle adventures.

Tracy Million Simmons and I are excited to deliver this issue to you, our third volume of true Kansas stories. These stories are written by Kansans and set in Kansas.

I was a youngster whose feet were, more often than not, pushing the pedals of her beloved teal-colored Western Flyer. But not everyone had the same joyful experience on two wheels. For some, bicycles are associated with difficulties or emotional trauma.

We were impressed with the wide variety of bicycle experiences—bikepacking, Biking Across Kansas, never owning a bicycle, anxiety, injury, competing in a triathlon.

In addition to the true bike stories, we have interviewed the invincible Kristi Mohn, an avid cyclist who has helped make Emporia the Gravel Grinding Capital of the World and who is making sure women have an equal place at the starting line.

As you read this issue, be thinking about what stories you might write for future editions. We are currently taking submissions (May 1 - June 30, 2022) for our food issue. Visit our website for more information: 105MeadowlarkReader.com.

If you are a subscriber or if you advertise in *105 Meadowlark Reader*, please know how much we appreciate your confidence in this journal and how much we value your support. You are 105's vital partners. You help make this print journal possible.

Onward,
Cheryl Unruh, editor
May 2022

Whoa

by Jerilynn Jones Henrikson

Daddy came home from the War when I was three years old. He moved in with Mom and me in the little blue Victorian house at 601 Exchange. (Don't bother searching. It was torn down several years ago.) I was not sure that he was actually part of the family, but he convinced me when he bought me a shiny new bicycle for my fourth birthday. Unfortunately, the bike was too big for me. The salesman had convinced Dad that it would be just right for a kid who was "almost five." Unfortunately, I was a shrimp, always at the end of the front row in every class picture.

A twelve-year-old boy who lived in the neighborhood became my hero, mainly because of his prowess as a bike rider. He delivered *The Emporia Gazette* daily, snatching the folded papers from a bag hanging on the handlebars and zinging them with gunslinger accuracy onto porches of subscribers up and down the elm-lined streets of his territory. I would put yesterday's news, clumsily refolded, into a paper bag and try to mimic his skill. No luck, what with awkwardly walking the bike down the sidewalk and stopping to balance the bike and throw the paper at the same time.

I also admired the way he came gliding home from school, sitting upright on the bicycle seat, arms folded across his chest, guiding the bike in graceful arcs with just the balance of his body. He could make a long, curving turn into his driveway! Every attempt I made to copy these maneuvers resulted in skinned elbows, or knees, or both.

When I was five, we left the little blue gingerbread house and my bike riding boy-god behind and moved to the country. The bike went with us. There were no sidewalks. The road past our house, indeed the roads throughout the entire rural hamlet of Plymouth, were all gravel. When I turned six, Dad said it was time to learn to ride my bike. On I got, with Dad running alongside holding on to the back of the seat. After several attempts, I found the balance point and picked up speed, leaving him behind cheering me on. "How do I stop?" I yelled.

"Pedal backwards!" he shouted. I slammed the brakes so hard, the momentum hurled me over the handlebars headfirst into the gravel road. Scalp wounds tend to bleed fast and hard. It looked and felt worse than it was. Afterward, I did pick little bits of gravel out of my scalp for several months. I also put the bike in the garage and talked my dad into getting me a palomino horse. My new hero had become Roy Rogers and his palomino, Trigger. Of course, the jury is still out on the wisdom of this trade-in, but, unlike most members of my family, I still prefer horses to bicycles.

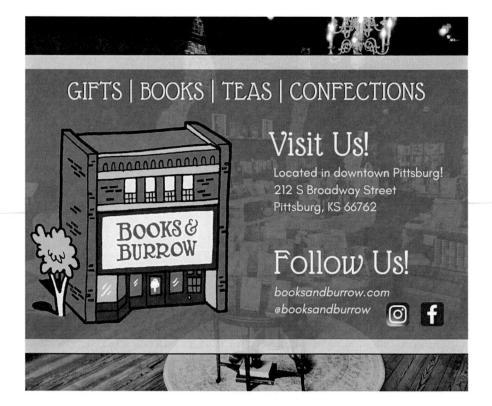

Miles to Go Before I Sleep
by Leon Unruh

At 5:30 AM on a July day in 1984, my friend Jane waited while I slid the front wheel into the fork of my 10-speed and closed the quick release. She wished me well and drove off toward the sunrise, back to Wichita. I was alone in the dark at the Oklahoma end of a 236-mile route north to Nebraska.

This was my dream day.

I had moved back to Kansas a year earlier and latched onto the flat and mostly empty county blacktops west of Wichita, seeing in them an old friend like the ones I had ridden as a teenager in Pawnee Rock. When the wind turned bitter, I put my brown-and-silver Raleigh on a training stand in the living room and built up my stamina while I faced a highway map spread out on the couch and imagined myself riding the next summer's Biking Across Kansas route.

It wasn't as if I were a novice. After graduating from KU in 1979, I took a newspaper editing job in Austin, Texas. I soon bought and modified the Raleigh Grand Prix and hit the Hill Country's back roads, sharing routes (but not times) with athletes training to become the US Olympic cycling team, among them Rebecca Twigg and Connie Carpenter, Davis Phinney and Eric Heiden.

In May 1981, I pedaled my naive self from Austin to Pawnee Rock, taking an 800-mile route covering eleven days: ten nights in cheap motels in Texas, western Oklahoma, and Coldwater, Kansas; an invitation to a humble rural family's Sunday dinner; and hearing a my-age oilfield worker describe his pleasure over shooting rattlesnakes near his pump jacks.

I expected an epiphany as I glided into Pawnee Rock—I also might have imagined a parade if I'd told anyone I was coming—but deep thoughts just didn't come. I was home in my old home, waiting for my sister's wedding that coming weekend. The day after I arrived, I pulled my jersey back on and rode to Larned, where I let my old editor at the _Tiller and Toiler_ talk me into being interviewed for a story.

In June 1984, I joined my brother-in-law on our first Biking Across Kansas, or BAK. We started out as talkative relatives but by the end were basically just two guys—different speeds, different goals—who might wave in passing. (He has since become part of a different family.) BAK's gift to me was teaching a pack of young riders mostly from Emporia and Americus to draft against the dry wind, muscle and fortitude against the weather. By the time we reached Missouri after eight days and about 500 miles, I was wondering how few days it'd take me to cross the state if I were to do it alone.

It'd take four or five days, I figured, to do the west-to-east route solo. But what if I crossed Kansas south to north? I hadn't heard of anyone doing that. Could I plan an efficient route avoiding cities but choosing a town, midway through the trip, large enough to have a motel?

My eventual route from the Oklahoma hamlet of Manchester rambled up paved county roads and minor highways, much of it along K-14. The biggest towns along the way were Anthony, Kingman, Sterling, Lyons, Ellsworth (a little over halfway), Lincoln, Beloit, and Jewell. After deciding on the route, my main hurdle was learning to beg for help—car rides to one state line and from the other and finding a safe place to sleep. I didn't want to burden my friends, but even more, I didn't want to weigh down my bike with a tent and sleeping bag.

I arranged to spend the night in Ellsworth with the gracious family of Jean Tanton, whom I'd met on BAK. When I said at their dinner table that I hoped I wouldn't run into any road construction north of town, her dad—a highway worker—set me straight about the value of laying asphalt under a hot sun. When I ran into a road crew the next morning up in the Smoky Hills, I regarded their work not with annoyance but with new respect, and yet I was still happy to outrun the oil's stench, which lingered for miles in the wind.

Days like that had few smells beyond cattle trucks and muddy creeks and the unyielding dismay of a distressed skunk. My pace fell into a rhythm, ninety or so pedal revolutions a minute in a high gear, gobbling up the yards, feeling the road's roughness up through the fork and handlebars and my funny mesh gloves, and working in a breezeless bubble when my road speed matched the tailwind. A half-hour, an hour, three hours: time didn't matter.

I loved cycling. Training brought me moments in the morning when I passed an irrigation-runoff ditch where redwing blackbirds clung to cattails and trilled like my brown wall phone, or the gold star I'd give myself after stretching my right leg over the bike frame to dismount after a hundred-mile round-trip for breakfast in the Kingman cafe.

And I feared cycling. It wasn't so much the possibility of hitting sand and flipping over an anonymous culvert where I'd land broken-legged in a gulch or being flattened by a car pushed aside by the draft from an 18-wheeler, although, of course, who doesn't dwell on those possibilities. (Once you learn to ride a bike, you never forget how to fall off one.) No, my fear had another father.

This was my deal: As a high schooler whose track coaches dumped me into the two-mile run for three years and didn't give me any coaching, I analyzed the quarter-mile lap times I'd need in order to win. I thought about it too much. I never made those times, never came close because competitive running was hard. I lettered for three years, but the stress became so bad that as a senior I traded my track spikes for the more cheerful path of chasing firetrucks to burning houses and selling photos of the fire to newspapers.

It was the fear of never being good enough, of not finishing, of failing my dreams. When I trained for my long rides, my mantra, keyed to pedal revolutions, was "Faster, harder, faster, harder." It grew into my nightmare.

But this week in July 1984 was sweet. Everything fit perfectly. If I went faster and harder, it was out of relief and the joy of a reunion with the Kansas of my memories.

The second day's ride ended in late afternoon at the Nebraska line just west of Superior, at the Republican River bridge. My friend drove out again from Wichita, helped me put my bike in the trunk, and drove me home. I was effervescent, in a dehydrated way, and newly convinced that the route could be done in a day.

After this solo crossing, I went to the Coventry Cycle shop in Wichita and picked up a $600 Italian racing frame—a beautiful blue Viner—and built a lighter, stiffer bike with new components geared for a one-day trip along my K-14 route. I increased my weekly training mileage to 300, 375, 400.

The shop's owner recommended a college-bound fellow from Newton who might agree to ride with me, and a tech guy in the shop and another rider offered to drive the sag wagon. To my regret, I do not remember the guys' names. The sag wagon, a van, was a necessity, given that at least an hour of riding would be sharing the road with highway-speed vehicles in the dark, and we needed blinking-light protection from behind.

The owner also tossed me a snug Coventry jersey, even though I would never be a racer. I felt sponsored, a team member, in the year of the Los Angeles Olympics.

As adventures go, the second Oklahoma-to-Nebraska run was free from stress. I didn't need to worry about being stranded or held up by a flat tire or running out of water. I was in top condition, and I had friends to ride with. Blowing through Kingman and Lyons and Ellsworth and Jewell, we accomplished the 236 miles in sixteen hours on August 8, 1984.

A couple of photos illustrate that summer. One, taken by Mrs. Tanton in Ellsworth, shows Jean and me standing comfortably close in their living room. Jean wears a white blouse and is proper and beautiful; I'm leaner and more tanned than I ever remember being, and irrepressibly happy. The second photo, from a month later, was taken out the sliding door of the sag wagon on the browned plains in Lincoln County, above Ellsworth. My riding partner leads by a yard or so as we effortlessly plug along. We aren't wearing helmets. I think 1984 was the last year I didn't sport a brain bucket.

In 2007, I rode BAK with my sons, Sam (11) and Nik (9), while my wife—whom I met on BAK 1985—drove a 24-foot camper as our informal sag wagon. We started in Colorado, west of Tribune, and came across on K-96 and K-4 to Hoisington before swinging up through Lincoln and Clay Center toward the northeast corner of the state. The boys were troupers, as long as they had popsicles. I asked Sam to set a pace of 13 mph, and he did so for hours on end until late in the trip when he was waylaid by a nasty patch of gravel and tossed into a ditch minutes before a thunderstorm swept in. Nik and I sometimes were the last to hit the town where BAK bedded down for the night, but we rode every foot of the way to the Missouri River at Elwood. I was told that he was the youngest to have completed BAK under his own power.

As young adults now on the verge of being on their own, my sons have their own near and distant goals, but at an early age they learned the value of putting one pedal ahead of the other on an endless road with a thunderstorm rising. They also hardly ever ride anymore.

In July 2014, working at the University of Alaska Fairbanks and by then divorced, I determined that I would run the Equinox Marathon. A much younger woman I dated for a while had run the previous year's race, and I wanted to prove to her, and myself, that I had the mettle to do it too. The course went over Ester Dome, a 2,364-foot mountain west of Fairbanks, in mid-September as golden autumn sped toward winter. Starting as a two-mile-a-morning dilettante, I built my mileage and hated my foolish pride every step of the way. "Faster, harder, faster, harder" roared back to life.

My race took more than six hours in the rain and fog. I badly misjudged the calories and stamina that, at 57, I needed just to walk fast after two hours of running uphill through the dark forest. There were missteps. I fell hard after I tripped on a birch root, and later I slid into a thigh-deep mudhole where the trail edged along a marsh. But I did finish, and a photo Nik took of me rounding the final turn is my proudest trophy. I will never have to look at Ester Dome and regret not finishing the toughest race I've ever run.

Two weeks after the marathon, a Fairbanks woman named Julie who saw my profile on Match.com verified my identity by looking up the bib number in that photo. She phoned, we met at the world's northernmost Denny's restaurant, and we've been together for seven years. Neither of us cares for running, but we're fond of bicycles. Julie often says, "The harder you work, the luckier you get," and that is true.

Leon Unruh: "The photo was shot out the side door of our sag wagon van as we pedaled north on K-14 in Lincoln County on August 8, 1984."

A classic is a book that has never finished saying
what it has to say.   Italo Calvino

Bicycles: A Love Story
by Boyd Bauman

I.

My first love came out of nowhere from my perspective. Actually, it likely came from a Nemaha County auction on a low bid, perhaps passed down through many older siblings first. A rusty one-speed farm bike, it was either blue paint peeling to red or vice versa. No brand, as this was the generic generation where kids rode "a bike" just like they wore "tennis shoes."

I ambushed Dad near dusk after he'd had another long day tending livestock and crops. In the corn stubble field east of the farmhouse, there were two tracks hardpacked by tractor and pickup. Dad held me steady for the briefest of moments, then gave a laborer's shove to get me over the top of the terrace.

Somehow, I balanced over the cloddy soil, but I couldn't steer. As I picked up speed, the bike slowly shanked toward the barbed wire fence between field and feedlot. I hit the taut wire and ricocheted off, holding it steady for a few more yards before bike and rider went down.

As I dusted off and inspected myself for puncture wounds, I glanced back to the starting line. Dad had already headed to the farmhouse, probably pulled off his cowboy boots by then.

The one and only lesson was finished. That's how I learned to ride a bike in Kansas. It hurt a bit, but I was hooked, and a romance began.

II.

My second love was the real deal. This was 1976, and no one I knew spoke of any sins committed by my country. Mom bought red, white, and blue plastic spoke covers for my wheels, and one could've heard them clatter clearly if I didn't have only rock and gravel roads to pedal down.

This was a bigger farm bike, clearly Massey Ferguson red. I could change speeds by standing up and pumping my fast-twitch preteen muscles. This was the bike that carried me to victory on Main Street of the Bern Day celebration in both the fast bike race *and* the slow bike race.

Big Red had a basket in which I carried a sword and shield made from the circular cardboard of a Tony's frozen pizza package. I'd bike a mile and a half to my classmate Pat's house, then we'd cruise to a bridge another mile or two down the road. Battles were staged under the bridge until, exhausted, we'd dip our toes in Turkey Creek.

These were the days kids were gone until suppertime, when Mom's supervision came in the form of, *Just look for the top of the silo if you get lost.*

As long as I avoided the grass burrs in the pasture, I could go as far as I wanted, as far as imagination would take me. My second love, it turns out, was the one that began to take me away from home.

III.

I admit I was unfaithful in high school and college. I'm so sorry. Oh, I was infatuated with noise and fossil fuels. We all were back then. I wanted to pick up girls, and when that went poorly, I held on to the *possibility* of picking up girls. These were confusing times, and I didn't have the wherewithal to relax and enjoy the ride. Please forgive me.

IV.

I fell for you again at 9,000 feet. A green and purple Trek Antelope 830. Early '90s model, and boy, would we get grungy! A Kansas boy's dream: to mountain bike in the mountains! We raced other ski bums, shifting and climbing 'til we were Rocky Mountain high on adrenaline. We vacationed in Moab. I had a single-track mind for you.

You were there for me the summer my CJ-5's engine went out, and we shared the most stunning commute of my working life. Silverthorne to Keystone Resort, bike path around Lake Dillon at sunrise and sunset.

Twenty-mile roundtrip with a thousand vertical feet at the end, but I was of a shape and an age that I simply geared down and filled my lungs with lower levels of oxygen.

You gave me chills. You took my breath away.

V.

Wanderlust guided me to the other side of the globe and into a temporary relationship with a loaner from the Higashi-Hiroshima Board of Education. A lovely lavender one-speed with a basket, you taught me there was no need for pretention, for machismo. Even CEOs in three-piece suits balancing briefcases pedaled to the train station. I accessorized with Velcro straps about the cuffs of my slacks to keep them unfrayed by the chain. You made me feel like a schoolkid again, navigating foreign roads on the way to class.

After a couple of years, I had booked a flight home to Kansas for a summer visit. One of my middle school English departments presented me with a decorative globe to take to my mom. Gift in bike basket, I made a quick stop at my Board of Education office on the way out of town. Five minutes later, my lavender beauty was gone, my mom's present resting on the pavement instead—a thoughtful gesture by a considerate Japanese thief.

I got another one-speed loaner upon my return, but I never forgot you. I thought I glimpsed you once near the 100 Yen Store, appearing smitten with another commuter, but not truly meaning it, I know. Perhaps our cross-cultural relationship wouldn't have held together for the long haul, but it was beautiful while it lasted.

VI.

I read Graham Greene's *The Quiet American* and fell in wanderlust again with the exotic. Forgive my bawdiness, but this romance was hot, was sultry, was wet. Soon I was pedaling another one-speed through Saigon—Paris of the East—a city of love.

One might believe the manic streets of Saigon would be as foreign as a setting could get for a boy from Kansas, but you should see what happens when your bike breaks down. Then you pull your vehicle off the road, and it isn't but a minute before someone runs up and looks it over. Something is said, someone else is whistled for, and a third person is summoned.

One may chalk it up to cutthroat capitalism in this communist country, but I saw a piece of Nemaha County *I-know-a-guy*. There was always that guy who could weld the swather, that guy who could by-guess-or-by-gosh his way around hydraulic lines of the scoop tractor. These were those indispensable men that Dad hoped would *last as long as I do.*

I recognized the men who worked in a flurry around my wounded bike to make it whole again. Their smiles were Midwestern nice. Ah, the amour I still feel for this scene. I knew these guys!

VII.

Whatever happened to that Colorado Trek and our breathtaking romance, you may wonder? My Antelope, gorgeous green and purple doe, actually moved to Kansas, where it has been through a number of changes. It navigated The Katy Trail, not with the speed and daring of its youth, but to keep pace with an intriguing companion.

It's been accessorized with child seats and a tag-along hitch. It survived a harrowing trip on I-635 in KCK when an updraft caught the attached kid's seat and threw my 21-speed beauty from the back of a pickup. Somehow, it bounced to a stop with only minor abrasions, waiting motionless in the fast lane of the interstate until I could exit and come back around. Faithful, as always.

Someday, God willing, it will pedal out of an empty nest. A bit slower, a bit creaky, maybe even a tad rusty. Yet, as it takes me forward, it will take me back. Back to a sultry Saigon night, an orderly Hiroshima commute, the crisp pine-scented air of 9,000 feet.

I may even feel the wind in my face from a Kansas farm field. Sense a dad behind me still giving a push.

Because that's what the great loves do for us, as you know. Make us feel like kids again. And this love, my two-wheeled romance, traverses terrain from origin story to break up to reconciliation. Yeah, it's a love that's built to last.

Death by a Banana Seat Bicycle
by Brandy Nance

I had to get there quick—to my best friend Alice's house on the outskirts of town to pick up money for her "flea medication." She had called me that morning, in a panic.

"I need you to pick me up some flea medication," she said frantically.

"Again?" I asked.

"Yes, I have fleas. I got it from my dog again," Alice said quietly.

It was 8:00 AM on a Saturday, a day my seventh-grade self normally would have happily slept until noon. I hastily threw the covers off my bed, not bothering to make it as I tiptoed out of the house to avoid having to explain anything to my mother and stepfather.

I hopped on my powder blue, banana seat bicycle and pedaled down the gravel road to her house to pick up the money. I arrived, tossed my bike aside, and ran up to the porch. Alice was already waiting for me behind the door; shy and embarrassed, she sheepishly handed the cash to me through a crack.

"Please hurry," she said. "I have to do this before my mother gets home. It's called Rid. If mom finds out, she'll make me get rid of the dog. Please don't tell anybody about this."

"I know what it's called," I said quietly.

As I took the money and returned to my bike, I knew what the medication was really for, and it had nothing to do with her wire-haired, yappy dog. It was the third time she had "fleas" that year, and her mother said if she got them again, she'd hold her down and shave her head bald. The thought of her having to go to school bald horrified me as I got back on my bike, pretending I was horseback riding to the pharmacy, pedaling as hard as I could to get the "flea medication."

As I pedaled, I imagined the sound of horse hooves and the flutter of dust being kicked up as we rode through a cow town, dodging the stagecoaches and women walking around in homemade dresses. The colorful tassels on my handlebars pelted my hands like reins around a horse's neck.

It was several blocks to the little pharmacy in small-town Wellington, which granted me a lot of time to indulge in my fantasy. Finally, my powder blue horse and I arrived at the pharmacy. I chained her to the bike rack and tiptoed to the aisle I had become familiar with. I quickly found what I wanted and took it to the counter.

"Again?" an old, plump man who always smelled like medication asked. He looked at me through thick glasses, his eyes appearing twice their size through the lenses.

I felt my face turn hot as I handed over the money and nodded.

"Someone should shave you bald," the man said as he handed me a bag with the medication in it, along with the change.

I felt sick. Even the old man at the pharmacy supported shaving a poor, bullied teen bald.

I ran out of the pharmacy and got back on my steed, but I no longer felt like pretending I was riding a horse. I pedaled as hard as I could to get to the outskirts of town and onto the gravel road. That's when everything went wrong. I took a nasty fall as I came onto the gravel road far too fast. I slid one way, my bike slid another way, and the medication flew into the ditch. I skidded on my left side to a stop, immediately feeling an ache in my shin. I looked down. Blood was pouring from my shin, and little pebbles seemed to be seeping out of my wound. Trying not to cry, I remembered I still had a mission to accomplish. I hurried to the ditch to search for the medication, which, after several minutes, was found, no longer in the bag. I picked it up, feeling the blood continue to seep out of my pebbly wound.

I retrieved my bike from the other side of the gravel road and carefully got back on, again pedaling fast, but not so fast I would repeat what had just happened. I imagined myself leaving a blood trail all the way to my friend's house. I wondered if I would bleed to death before I got there, and Alice would be forced to have her head shaved. Monday she would go to school bald, mocked by the kids who already called us "The Losers Club." She'd be bald and mourning her best friend who died in a tragic bike accident while delivering her "flea medication." And if I didn't die, I imagined myself being taken to the hospital to get a skin graft. But first they'd have to pull all the tiny pebbles out of my leg and then take the skin from my other leg to fix my skinned leg.

I pedaled harder before all the blood drained out of my body and Alice couldn't get her medication. I began to cry. I didn't want to die delivering "flea medication" on the back of my banana seat bike that everyone made fun of anyway. I could imagine them printing it in the school paper: Brandy, leader of "The Losers Club," dies while riding her banana seat bike with babyish tassels on the handlebars.

Finally—after what seemed like hours and gallons of blood (I wondered how much blood a human body could possibly lose and still live)—I made it to Alice's house where I tossed my blood-soaked bike aside and hobbled to her porch. Alice was again waiting by the door, this time opening it wide when she saw I was crying. She looked alarmed.

I handed her the slightly beat up box of Rid.

"I'm bleeding!" I said, trying not to sob. "I'm bleeding everywhere. I might die."

Alice looked at my leg, which was covered in a mix of blood and gravel and shook her head.

"You're not going to die," she said, giggling.

"It's not funny!" I said. "I'm going to bleed to death!"

"Get in here," Alice said. "But don't bleed on the carpet. Wait, let me get you a paper towel. My mom will kill me if you get blood everywhere."

"But someone needs to take me to the hospital," I insisted. "Maybe we should call 9-1-1 right now."

"Good God, no, you don't need to go to the hospital," Alice said, stifling another laugh.

Alice disappeared for a second, returning with a handful of paper towels, which I applied to my leg, and I followed her into the bathroom where we had done two other "flea" treatments.

"Sit in the tub," Alice said. "Let's clean it off."

I took my place in the bright green tub and Alice came over to inspect my wound.

"Gross!" she exclaimed. "You have rocks under your skin!"

I felt like throwing up.

"See, I need to go to the hospital," I said. "They need to do surgery and take them out."

"Stop!" Alice said. "You're not going to the hospital."

Alice ran some water on another handful of paper towels and started washing off my shin. It stung.

"Hey, that hurts!" I said.

"Well, then you do it," she snapped. "Get out of the tub so I can wash my hair before mom gets here. You'll need to help me get the flea eggs out."

As she undressed, I noticed bruises on her arms that were previously covered by her long-sleeved shirt. I knew not to ask about them, but I understood where she got them, which was why this process was so urgent, even if I was bleeding to death in her bathroom.

I sat on the toilet, cleaning off my leg while she showered. I had no idea how I'd get the rocks out of my leg, but at least the bleeding wasn't so bad. I was finally able to tell myself that I wasn't going to bleed to death and that my legacy wouldn't be "death by a banana seat bicycle." I imagined my mother's shame after I died that way and not a more fantastic accident.

"Alice, how am I going to get the pebbles out of my leg?" I asked.

"Get some tweezers and dig them out," she said.

It was at that point I swore I was going to burn my bike when I got home. I suddenly hated the thing.

I rummaged through the medicine cabinet until I found a pair of tweezers and I began to dig under my skin, pulling out tiny pebbles.

"Put some peroxide on that, too," Alice said, as she turned the water off. "Hand me a towel."

I handed her a towel and turned my attention back to my leg, digging the last few pebbles out of it.

"That's going to leave a nasty scar," Alice said, as she got out of the shower. I noticed she tried to shift the towel to hide more bruises on her body.

I nodded as I poured peroxide on it, feeling the sting as it bubbled on my skin. Yes, I was definitely going to burn my bike when I got back home.

I stood up to rummage for some bandages, finally finding several that I stuck all over my wound.

"That's really going to hurt when you go to take those off," Alice said.

"Well, if I had gone to the hospital, they could have given me a proper-sized one," I snapped.

Alice handed me the tiny comb, and I began to comb the eggs out of her hair, carefully putting them on a paper towel that we would flush down the toilet so her mom wouldn't see.

"I'm sorry you fell," Alice said.

"I'm going to burn my bike when I get home," I said. "I never want to ride it again."

"That's just silly," Alice said. "Why would you burn your bike?"

I said nothing and continued to comb eggs out of her hair, suddenly realizing my scrape was nothing as I stared at the bruises on her body.

Real Men Make Quiche
by Edgy Sack

"I'll make quiche." These are the words I never, not once, heard my husband, Chris, utter . . . before now.

Sally, one of our daughters, didn't miss a beat.

"Great," she said, "what time should we all come? I'll bring fancy fruits."

This meant maybe blackberries or blueberries would be included. It had been less than two weeks since my husband was in a bicycle accident, a bad crash that had cost him his pinky.

No matter that his knees, forearms, and elbows were wrapped with bandages, this was Mother's Day he was talking about. And I was not about to ask, "How are you going to make a quiche without a pinky?"

After all, he had taken the grandkids fishing twice since it happened, cooked wieners and brats on an open fire, s'mores too, and had already ridden his bike to the repair shop, sans pinky.

That's one of the things I love about him; he never gives up. When he fell off a ladder and broke his back, he hobbled along the sidewalk wearing his "turtle shell" brace, pushing a walker with tennis balls, a bit more each day until he regained his strength. He never complains. He lets you know it hurts, but he pushes himself back. He did the same thing when he went over the handlebars of the same bike a few years ago, breaking his collar bone after failing to stop at a stop sign, and then having to stop for a car in the middle of the street. Oops!

With the collar bone accident, a retired nurse called me to inform me he was en route to the hospital. With his pinky, the woman who called me was a "registered nurse." Her words, some of the first out of her mouth.

"Hello, I'm a registered nurse, who is this I am talking to?" she yelled. I knew she was yelling out to Chris, my husband, because I heard him moaning.

I screamed into the phone, "This is his wife. I'm his wife, what happened?"

"He's had a bad accident; he's lost a finger. I don't think he hit his head," she shouted into the phone. "The ambulance is coming."

"Don't take him to Providence," I shouted back to her.

In perfect nurse fashion, she said, "I don't think I can dictate where he goes."

"Yes, you can, and do it!"

"Ok, I'll make sure the ambulance drivers call you and let you know where they take him to."

Before all this I had just sat down in the den chair with a glass of sugar-free grape Kool-Aid, my favorite. We were watching two of the grandchildren while their parents were scoping out a place to live twelve hours away to finish some schooling. I had a three-year-old napping and a six-year-old resting upstairs.

"Where did he crash?" I asked the registered nurse. "I have little ones I am watching, and I have to get one of my daughters to come be with them." The street she told me was sixteen blocks from the house.

"He's okay," she said. "The ambulance is on the way, I'm sure."

The rain was falling heavier. Lightning and thunder were crashing through the sky. When the phone rang, I thought he was calling me because it had started raining, really raining, to tell me he was being rained on. I had told him before he left, "I hope you can beat the rain because I can't rescue you today." He thought he could beat the rain.

Now it was pouring. I dialed my daughter that was the closest in proximity. "Dad crashed; he lost a finger." I ran up the stairs.

"I'll be right there. I'm buckling the baby in now."

I stuffed shorts, underwear, socks, t-shirt, and his shoes into a Target bag. My daughter arrived, her eight-month-old in her arms. She touched my arm gently but firmly and said, "It's going to be okay, Mom."

"Annie's coming, I called her two times in a row, and she answered." That little "code" had been established in a previous "emergency." We were downstairs again. I went back up and got the six-year-old. "Papa has had a bike crash. He lost a finger. Gigi has to go to him. You won't be alone. Sally and Annie are coming to stay with you." I don't know what possessed me to blurt out the part about the lost finger to a six-year-old.

Audrey, the six-year-old, yelled out as soon as she saw Sally, "Papa's finger fell off!"

A white truck with lights on pulled up in the side drive; a man popped out, ran around to the bed of the truck, and pulled Chris's bike off and rolled it to the back yard. I hollered at him from the door through the now torrential rain and motioned for him to come in. He ran for the door, head down. His name was Shannon. "He's hurt bad, he's really bad, he's doing a lot of moaning. I saw him rolling around in the road and cars were racing past him. No one was stopping, so I did a U-turn, and used my truck as a shield for him." He pulled a business card from his wallet. "I want someone to call me and let me know how he is. Please call."

"Okay. Thank you sooo much." I hugged his wet person.

At this point Sally said, "Mom, you cannot take this bag to the hospital. Get a real bag." She was right, so I went back up the stairs. She followed, baby in arms, Audrey trailing. "Don't forget things you will need, too. Your contact case and snacks and underwear. You might be there a while."

I pulled the black backpack out of Chris's closet and tied his shoes to the strap like we did when we went on trips, and put his shirt, underwear, socks, and shorts in the middle pocket. I removed the sharpies and pens and put my toothbrush and contact things in. I pulled panties and a fresh shirt from my closet. After coming down the stairs, Sally reminded me again that I had to have snacks.

As I packed up, my phone rang.

"Where are you?"

"They took me to KU Med."

"I'll be there soon."

"My pinky is gone."

"I'm sorry, I'll be there soon."

The rain was coming down in sheets.

"Oh good, Annie's here." Sally yelled this up the basement stairs. "You drive her, Annie. She can't drive in this." Audrey had been following Sally around, jumping up and down to amuse the baby and feeding her graham crackers. Annie turned around on the stairs and we ran to her car in the driveway.

I must admit, as soon as I heard which finger it was, I started breathing again. When they let me in the emergency room, Chris's color looked good. He was bandaged and under blankets. There was a policeman standing near the bed with his back to me. I thought, *Did Chris break the law? Is it illegal to crash a bike?* The policeman introduced himself and told me he had seen Chris many times on his bike, and he was going to investigate this as a hit and run.

I didn't dare look at his hand but, on his blankets, at his feet, I saw the pink Ziploc bag with ice holding his pinky finger. I thought, *No way. Is that how they carry stuff? In Ziploc bags with ice?*

"They are going to try and reattach my finger," he said. "I'll have to stay in ICU for four days."

That's going to be some lonely days, I thought, *but that finger doesn't look like it's going anywhere but in the trash.*

Our son-in-law, who is in med school, kept texting us. "Get that finger reattached—stat!"

I had no idea what "stat" meant, but I had a strong feeling stat was not on anyone's mind in the emergency room. The nurse pulled open the curtain, handed Chris a clipboard, and told him to sign several papers giving them permission to operate. The pinky that was gone was on his right hand, the one he writes with. He signed. That was my first time to look at his hand. It was bandaged up poorly and the bandage was soaked with blood.

The nurse said to me, "Could we get you to leave the room now and wait in the waiting room?"

A man was shouting out in the waiting room and rolling himself on the floor occasionally. I kept thinking, *of course they are going to come and get me.* After a few minutes, I went around to the only door they would let you go through. It was very chaotic, lots of shouting and foul words. They were getting ready to wheel Chris to surgery.

"This is a hand surgeon, right?" I asked.

They told me I could follow him to the surgery door and say my goodbyes there. I waited in the waiting room, COVID-style. Sally was right. No water, no snack machines, quite unfriendly. I heard this was going to be at least a four-hour surgery, maybe longer. In less than forty minutes, my name was called and a man that looked to be a surgeon, who had a fanny pack on, motioned for me to follow him.

We went in the room where they take a person for privacy. "Well, we went ahead and amputated. You know he ripped it off in the bicycle chain, so it wasn't a clean cut."

Of all the things I could have gotten upset about that day, this was the one statement where I found my voice. "That is impossible. The chain did not rip his finger off. It couldn't have happened that way. It had to be the gear shift, he would have had to contort his body to have a chain do that and he wouldn't have pedaled his own pinky!"

Either way, his pinky was gone.

"They'll be out shortly to get you; they are waking him up."

An aide came looking for his clothes. I handed her the backpack with the shoes tied to it.

I discussed with the man across from me in the waiting room the impossibility of what the surgeon had said. He agreed with me. Then I heard Chris laughing in the hallway. The nurse rolling him out said to me, "He only needed help with his shoes, otherwise he dressed himself. He's got some pretty bad road burns, and he is going to hurt."

As we stood outside waiting for Sally to pick us up, he said to me, "They made me repeat four times that it was highly likely that I would wake without a finger. I guess I did. I'm sure going to miss that finger."

It was still drizzling as we said thanks and goodbye to the nurse. She said to me, "You've got a real keeper there," nodding towards Chris.

In the end, I know he would have liked to have kept his finger, but that quiche was the best I have ever eaten, made by a man whose finger was cut off in a bike chain.

They Traded My Horse for a Bicycle
by Anne Spry

My six-year-old-self regarded the shiny new bicycle with suspicion.

I was not getting on that thing. Not even after someone attached the training wheels as an afterthought. Their original flawed thinking must have held that a child who could saddle a horse and ride all over twenty acres by herself could easily adapt to a bicycle.

They were quite mistaken.

The cynical, worldly child I had become could already feel the sting of freshly embedded gravel in my knees from falling off that contraption I was supposed to be excited about. Besides, bicycles were for city kids who lived in neighborhoods with smooth sidewalks and concrete driveways. We lived in the country with a long gravel drive winding past a row of young trees with white-washed trunks and on back to several outbuildings. That twenty acres on 45th Street near Forbes Airfield would eventually be swallowed up by the encroaching city of Topeka. It was destined for reincarnation as a go-cart track and for other commercial property uses. But before my new blue bike made it on the scene in 1954—apparently in a trade for my beloved old mare Bullet—it had been a magical place for a Kansas youngster to grow and explore.

I spent hours in the barn loft, with its lingering scent of alfalfa hay and its two massive open doors—one looking south toward Wakarusa and the farmstead my dad had left to start his aggregate lime business. But the north door got most of my attention, especially at night when I could gaze toward the "metropolis" and search out the dome of the capital building.

That wonderful loft, empty of hay during our tenure, was the perfect place to roller skate. Or to crawl up into by using a ladder worn smooth in the middle by previous feet. I had to scale it carefully, with one hand, because the other one usually held my favorite tiger-stripe kitten, Cookie. It was such a great place to daydream. I spent many solitary hours up there, pretending to be Annie Oakley (one of my nicknames— I preferred it to the more negative one of Twister) lying in wait for desperados I had chased on my horse Bullet, named after the TV Annie's horse. I hatched detailed plans in my reveries about how I would drop down on the unsuspecting criminals from the hole in the floor of the loft.

My second daydreaming space on our twenty acres led me through a different kind of imaginary scenario. There, in a long building we called the boathouse, I traded my rural western daydreams for potential urban fame as a concert pianist and/or singer. Instead of housing a boat, this building boasted only a decrepit upright piano, with the ivories peeled off most of the keys and mice nesting in the felt strikers. I spent hours pounding on the woefully out-of-tune keys, composing child concerts, and singing, pausing only when I had exhausted myself. During intermissions from the dissonant concerts, I would try to capture the dust motes that lifted on shafts of sunlight piercing the cracks in the weathered wood walls. I didn't know then that they were nothing but dust; didn't have the vocabulary to name those sun-lit particles. To me they were magical, and I tried to bottle the motes like summer fireflies. I tried to taste them by grabbing at them with my grubby fists and then opening my hands into my mouth. I was so disappointed when I could only taste sweaty-palm salt or something that reminded me of the toe jam I had dug out of my feet before last night's bath.

When the bicycle made its appearance, I hadn't been in the boathouse or the barn in weeks. It seemed like forever ago since I'd caught the pungent scent of horse sweat mixed with manure, heard the swish of oats in a feed bucket, or brushed a tangled mane while smoothing the soft, reddish-brown hair on my best friend.

I didn't want a stupid bike. I just wanted my Bullet back. Had they sold my gentle old mare because of that last wild ride I took back to the barn over a freshly oiled 45th Street? Yes, I had ruined a saddle. But I paid for that sin by being humiliated and forced to take a bath in a galvanized tub filled with kerosene—outdoors—in front of everybody.

And the whole thing wasn't even my fault. It was that woman who was riding with me—a twenty-something blonde airhead who had never been on a horse. She must have been involved somehow with that Air Force colonel who owned the Palomino we were boarding on our farm. In fact, Forbes Air Base had been a great source for boarding horses and trailer lot renters. Two house trailers were parked behind our white frame home—one owned by an Air Force family and the other by an older couple. The lot rent and horse boarding fees helped support us now.

Ross and Helen Johnson lived in one of the trailers, and when Ross wasn't working at a nearby quarry, the childless couple spent a lot of time with my brother Jim and me. He showed me everything he knew about horses. Taught me how to curry comb Bullet and even how to saddle her. Ross was probably even responsible for the gift of Bullet in the first place.

The Johnsons had taken me and Jim into their mobile home and their hearts from the moment they moved onto our place. They came soon after Daddy died and after our mom had to go to work driving his gravel and lime trucks. My mother must have needed the extra money and we needed the couple's attention. Helen became our resident babysitter and we enjoyed regular meals at the Johnson trailer (except for Helen's Czechoslovakian ruble soup and her stewed tomatoes and scrambled eggs . . . yuck!).

Despite always feeling loved by the Johnsons, I was now mystified about how my Bullet had been taken away one day and replaced with a bicycle.

Even as a six-year-old, I knew it wasn't like Ross Johnson to allow an inexperienced rider to get on that spirited horse that day. He must have assumed that my lack of fear around the stallion (I could walk between his legs and behind him without fear) would make up for this woman's lack of experience. I had already ridden the horse by myself once . . . without permission.

After Daddy was killed, I had our twenty acres and outbuildings mostly to myself. No one noticed the day I coaxed the Colonel's horse near the board fence next to the barn. I had somehow managed to pre-position my saddle on the top rung. With a lot of nervous, heavy breathing and no small amount of fear, I wrangled the saddle onto the cream-colored animal, then crawled underneath to fasten the cinch. This was a procedure I always accomplished by myself with Bullet, whose swayed back and gentle nature made it easy for a six-year-old. But that day I had forgotten to put a blanket under the saddle I finagled onto the stallion. And I was way too short to put reins on a horse that was seventeen hands high or even take off his halter. I just wanted to ride that beautiful beast and see if he would go faster than Bullet.

And ride we did that day! I felt every bit like the real Annie Oakley. I had my toy six-shooters with me and was appropriately dressed in the same western denim costume I'd worn for a dance recital with my classmates at Bruce Private School. The long leather tassels that fastened the metal embossed stars of my vest blew up, slapped, and stung my face on that ride, while my pigtails fanned out behind me. The Palomino's hooves stirred the sweet smell of alfalfa underneath me and I held on tightly to the pommel, laughing in pure joy at the freedom I felt riding so much faster than Bullet's usual canter. This was a true gallop, and it perfectly matched the pace of my glorious daydreams.

I got in trouble when we got back to the barn; scolded for taking that horse out by myself, without reins. Didn't I know that if something happened and that expensive horse tripped or got hurt, we'd have to pay the Colonel to replace his magnificent animal? Or at least pay the vet bill?

But days later, when that woman got to ride the Palomino instead of me, my daydreams were dashed to ruins. I stuck out my lower lip in a pout about being stuck on slow-pokey Bullet. But then halfway down 45th Street, my best-friend horse surprised me by galloping behind the stallion, nearly matching his dead run through the road oil.

I guess my mother and Ross must have blamed Bullet and me for not being able to control that Palomino and his cargo of blonde inexperience. Things were going to change. I heard something whispered between the two of them about a glue factory. The next day I went to feed Bullet her oats, but she was gone.

When I threw a six-year-old temper tantrum, they led me to the machine shed. They showed me that bike.

"I just want my horse," I wailed, kicking gravel dust into the spokes of the metal thing on wheels. I refused to mount it. I didn't trust wheels. I wanted hooves to be under me, not aluminum spoked wheels.

They held a whispered conference out of my earshot. Then they left me there with that bike, with its two big wheels and two little ones. I pouted all the way to the house and went to bed without supper, sobbing. I lay face down on my twin bed, repeating what had become a nightly ritual. First my left leg bent from the knee and pounded down on the mattress, causing the bedsprings to squeak. Then the right leg came down. Squeak. Smack. Squeak. Smack.

The cadence usually lulled me to sleep and quieted the voices above my head—voices that I likened to the rustle of brown paper bags. I didn't know then that my father and my angels were probably holding a conference about and above me, just like my mother and Ross had been behind me and out of earshot.

On some nights I woke up with a start and rubbed my eyes furiously with my fists. I tried to blot out the nightmare by putting enough pressure on my eyeballs to replace the terror of the bad dream with sparkling stars of myriad colors. Had the wreck I just witnessed been right outside our house? Or was I somehow witnessing the accident that had killed my father? I didn't understand dreams or nightmares. Didn't really understand life at all. Didn't have the vocabulary to name loss or grief.

From the age of four–when my father's dump truck was hit head on by an overloaded truck speeding away from the Gerlach Construction Materials quarry—to the age of six and the day the bicycle showed up to replace my horse—I had trouble distinguishing between nightmares and reality. Only recently did I learn, from a newspaper clipping handed to me by an aunt, that the accident occurred at the rural intersection of South California Street and old Berryton Road. My aunt also filled in details I would have preferred never to hear, even with my adult ears—

that my father's skull was crushed under the wheels of his own truck after the impact caused him to be ejected onto the gravel road. My six-year-old self would not have known or cared that his funeral was one of the biggest ever held in Topeka. But my adult self longed to listen to the story and learn that so many people loved my dad because of his light-hearted, teasing ways and his genuine concern and interest in others. The day they buried him, on my fourth birthday, may have been the day I started pouting . . . the day I began having nightmares . . . and the day a four-year old started wearing perpetually sad eyes.

My father's accident was probably why I didn't trust my bicycle. A new hunk of metal on wheels could never make up for the loss of Daddy's teasing pull on my pigtails or the way he pretended to gobble my neck when I was sitting on his lap. When Bullet came into my life, at least her warm, graying muzzle and soft lips reminded me of my father's tender touches. At least she was flesh and blood and bones with a soft hide to run my hands over.

I don't remember ever learning to ride that bicycle. And I have no recollection of the bike being strapped into the bed of my mother's new pickup as we pulled away from Kansas one day. My mother and brother and I were headed to a new life in a trailer park in Tulsa, Oklahoma, the pickup towing a 55-foot Nashua house trailer that would become our home on wheels. We left our house on 45th Street, with its screened-in porch and wonderful, knotty-pine lined attic playroom. We left my cousins, aunts, uncles, and both sets of grandparents behind to forge a new life.

We left furtively to escape from the sociopath that my mother had replaced my father with. He had been threatening to cut Jimmy and me into pieces with his pocketknife and make her watch. I knew he could do it, and so did she. He had already beat me with a belt until my back was bloody and bruised, just because he thought I had broken a glass measuring cup on one of the whitewashed tree trunks outside our house. My brother did that, but it didn't matter. That mean man was just darn proud of how well he could parent and punish because he showed his handiwork to my mother, roughly yanking up my shirt to expose a bruised, bloodied back.

We got away from him, but the wheels on our new home never grounded us. In fact, not too many months after spending a hungry winter in Tulsa, we were forced by flood waters to pull that Nashua back to Kansas and park it on my grandparents' acreage near Auburn. That's where I attended third grade. I can remember my third-grade teacher, but I don't remember the bicycle. I doubt I could have ridden it on the gravel drive anyway. For fun, I spent hours running up and down my grandpa's wooden cattle loading shoot and trying to approach one of his Black Angus steers to see if its hair felt anything like I recalled Bullet's feeling.

I don't think I got on a two-wheeled anything again until I tried to ride my brother's Honda 250 and promptly wrecked it in our yard. I was in college then and had come home for the summer. The Honda scared me just as my first and only bike did. I didn't trust the wheels, or myself to avoid a wreck.

I did manage to conquer my fear of bicycles by the time I became a mother and fastened a kiddie seat to the back of a garage sale model. I carried my son all over the bumpy asphalt roads of the small town where we lived. But I don't think he trusted me any more than I trusted myself or the bike. Even at the age of four he probably picked up on my dry-mouthed fear of two wheels through the tensed muscles of my back as we rode—supposedly for his fun and my own exercise.

When my son grew up and went away to college, I let his stepdad talk me into buying his and hers mountain bikes and all the paraphernalia that went with the off-road sport. We never really rode them much. They were status symbols intended to disguise our out-of-shape, sedentary lifestyles. They stayed in the garage on ceiling hooks—better to look at than use. My husband had replaced his beloved, decked-out Yamaha 750 with the mountain bikes and a Miata convertible. But that was only after I rode on the back of his motorcycle one day and leaned the wrong way, nearly causing it to lay it down on asphalt.

My husband and I had family accidents in our common book of experiences. His father had nearly killed his older sister on the back of a motorcycle. After emerging from a nine-month coma, she had to learn to talk and walk again. But she never fully recovered and walked with a cane until older age, when she graduated to spending her days seated in a contraption with two big wheels and two little ones.

I eventually learned to push through my fears and beyond my comfort zone where two-wheeled things are concerned. But I never truly learned to trust myself to not keel over the way that character on the tricycle always did in the 1960s comedy show *Laugh-In*. And I never got over having my horse replaced by a bicycle.

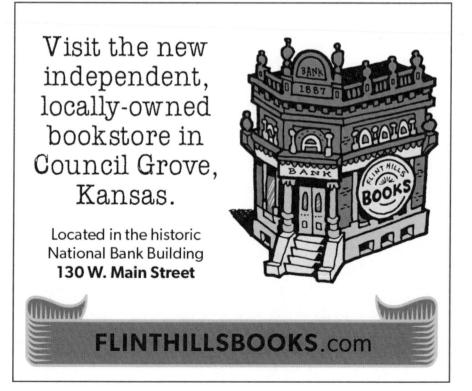

A Rolling Start
by Peg Nichols

I rarely asked for anything. Money was tight. I couldn't believe my ears when my mother said that I shouldn't count on it as a sure thing, but she might be getting me a bicycle. She was so tentative I responded with little enthusiasm.

"Don't get your expectations too high," she warned. "It won't be a new, sparkling, shiny bike." She explained, rather vaguely, that it was an old, well-worn bicycle that a family who was planning to move might decide wasn't worth taking with them. I had almost forgotten until one afternoon—surprise—I found an old, decrepit, paint-free, no-fenders bicycle leaning against the side of our little house.

I grabbed the handles and pulled the bicycle away from the wall. I had never ridden a bike before—what was I supposed to do? It was a boys bike. I threw my left leg over the frame and stood, fixed in place, both feet firmly on the ground, wondering how I was ever going to get in motion. Suddenly, I had an audience. All my neighborhood playmates and their siblings had gathered to watch. I lifted my feet, intending to place them on the pedals. I began immediately to tilt. My feet went instantly back on the ground.

With a feeling of fear and dread sinking down into my stomach, I looked around for Byron Reynolds. Byron had been a recent source of amusement and merriment as he snatched his older brother's bike and attempted to learn how to ride. His brother in hot pursuit, Byron regularly crashed into a garage door, a tree, a fence, or any nearby obstacle. Was Byron about to get a morsel of revenge? I closed my eyes, hoping they would all magically vanish.

"The hill," Shirley Reynolds, an older sister, shouted, "Go down the hill," and began running toward one of the two driveway entries into our little village. Dubious, I swung my leg free of the frame and began walking the bike to the top of the gradual slope. Astride the frame again, I lifted my feet and let the bicycle gently glide some sixty feet to a more level section. Maintaining balance was amazingly simple. My legs dangled on both sides. I loved the feel of the breeze in my hair. When the bicycle coasted to a stop I dismounted and made my way back to the top. Once more downhill. I was beginning to enjoy this.

The third time someone yelled, "Pedal." My feet found the pedals and almost automatically began turning. I was moving on my own. I applied a little pressure and increased the speed ever so slightly. I was in control. As easy as that.

I've ridden other, fancier bicycles, some as an adult, but I've never forgotten the power of that moment when I felt the strength of my legs transfer into motion and shoot me forward. As easy as that. But the most enduring lesson of all was learning that every undertaking has a better chance at success if you can get a rolling start.

@mikedyephoto   Instagram Facebook Twitter   mikedyephoto.com

What I Learned from Riding the Bicycle
by Amy Deckert Kliewer

"Let me remark to any young woman who reads this page that for her to tumble off her bike is inexcusable. The lightsome elasticity of every muscle, the quickness of the eye, the agility of motion ought to preserve her from such catastrophe. I have had no more falls simply because I would not. I have proceeded on a basis of the utmost caution and aside from that one pitiful performance the bicycle has cost me hardly a single bruise."

—Frances E. Willard,
How I Learned to Ride the Bicycle

(Frances E. Willard decided to learn
to ride the bicycle at the age of 53 in 1892.)

Frances Willard wrote in her book about the freedom and delight she enjoyed by learning to ride the bicycle. I can certainly relate to those feelings, but I don't consider falling a fault. My experience on the bicycle was indeed one of freedom and joy, and I took many spills and acquired numerous scrapes and bruises. Unlike Frances, I always tested my limits and tried to keep up with my friends. I did not pause to consider the consequences and only briefly glanced at my surroundings before flying down the road, alley, sidewalk, or ditch. No obstacle seemed insurmountable.

Growing up in the small town of Pawnee Rock in western Kansas in the '60s and '70s, we walked or bicycled for transportation. We rode everywhere. My single-speed bike took me around town but also through the country to the river or the creek. We loved to coast down the half-mile hill from The Rock (Pawnee Rock) with the wind blowing our hair. I felt like such a daredevil when I let loose of the handlebars. At the bottom of the hill, we rode down a deep ditch and back out in a preliminary form of dirt biking. I learned to trust myself and my ability to land upright as I came out on the other side of the ditch. I also learned that bloody knees did not have to stop me. I did envy my friend with her banana seat and high handlebars. Her bike with its lower point of gravity seemed to be able to take the dips and curves with greater ease than mine.

We also played a traveling version of hide and seek on our bicycles, ringing our bells to give clues to our location. We considered few areas off-limits and ducking through alleys was common. Sound echoed off brick buildings and cast doubt on distance and location.

A favorite game I played with my friend and constant companion involved riding double on our bikes around the school playground. We took turns pedaling while the rider closed their eyes. On their honor to keep them closed, the passenger squealed in fear as the person pedaling rode around the swing sets, slipper-slide, jungle gym, and teeter totter. The driver delighted in trying to trick the rider and disorient them by swerving suddenly or gradually veering off course. The ability to imagine accurately the distance and bearing of each obstacle challenged us. As the blind rider, I knew that obstacles loomed in our path. The shadows of the structures played across my eyelids, and I cringed. I wanted to jump off before we crashed. This exercise required that we trusted the other person enough to enjoy the sense of danger without succumbing to the temptation to peek. Absolutely sure that the jungle gym lay directly in our path, we maintained our balance and composure by holding onto the belief that the driver would not want to injure themselves or damage their bike.

One summer, I babysat for three young boys with much energy and imaginations. I quickly discovered that the key to a successful day involved riding our bikes. I learned that sitting with them at home could lead to activities that were difficult to control or distract from. Our best days involved exploring the creeks on our bikes. I carried our sack lunches hanging from my handlebars. We explored the water and the creek banks as we studied insects, tadpoles, frogs, and fish. We waded barefoot and felt the cool mud squish between our toes. Those days went by quickly and expended the boys' energy. They also fueled my love of exploration.

In western Kansas, the strongest obstacle to riding my bike anywhere was the wind. The wind often felt like my enemy, my antagonist. It whirled, prickled, stung, whipped, and buffeted me. It sometimes overwhelmed me. But the wind also embodied my restless spirit constantly whirling inside my chest. I wanted to be set free from the confines of the small town and limits of society. I wanted to push back against the forces of nature and community. I could relate to Frances Willard in this regard.

Later, I traded my bicycle for a car. Against the wind, it took me further, but it didn't set me free. At college and in my career, I bucked resistance other than the wind. Sometimes I could observe it, and sometimes I still imagined the obstacles looming in front of me. Remembering the lesson from riding double, I tried to maintain my balance and composure. I pushed forward and hoped I stayed upright.

The joy of freedom instilled, and the courage gained by the early adventures on my single-speed bike carried throughout my life. I searched for new adventures which usually involved travel and exploration. I explored career paths and pursued civil engineering. The obstacles were both real and imagined. I tried to balance my desire for adventure with restraint, sometimes with success, but I "bloodied my knees" more than a few times.

In recent years, I have dusted off my interest in cycling. Wet, muddy trails still sometimes claim my elbows and knees. Living in Kansas, wind resistance seems ever-present but not insurmountable. Again and again, I remind myself that I can trust in myself and my bicycle.

Books.
Community.
Fighting for a better world.
Cats.

Where I Like
by Julie Ann Baker Brin

There were basically two avenues to freedom for a farm kid outside a small town: sunsets and bicycles.

Dreaming big under wide skies after a miles-long ride (we were allowed to go three whole miles from home) with Jill, my Wonder Twin (powers, activate!), was the perfect way to spend a summer evening if there was still enough light and nobody was hollering our names.

Of course, we weren't twins, or even related—just best friends by proximity, guilty of watching perhaps a few too many of the same after-school specials or Saturday morning cartoons. There were only five channels in the middle of a "Population 23" township; take that as evidence we definitely weren't spoiled. But somehow, miraculously, we also weren't bored. And, of course, a few miles just happened to be the size of our "block" in rural America. But it was an entire solar system to us.

Ah, sweet freedom.

Little did we realize every home on the path of our orbit was a potential surveillance satellite for neighbors reporting to our mothers any untoward behavior that might have been witnessed. (I'm not inclined to say whether any of them were using rotary phones—after all, one doesn't ask about a lady's age!) But our own parents could eyeball us most of the way anyway, as long as the fields didn't have corn (or those that did weren't yet as high as an elephant's eye).

Making the rounds included hours of playing in The Ditch, stomping around on generous dirt banks flanking the jumpable "crick" between cool concrete arched footings supporting the road above us. It was our favorite hangout when it wasn't preempted by stinky boys from down the road. Looking back now, I can't believe we got away with spending so much time there, underneath a fairly busy thoroughfare leading to a state reservoir. Evidently the next generation agreed, because now there's an enclosed culvert and official signage—no more hand-scrawled proclamations of "[Cousin] Pat is a [wordy dird]," or "Julie loves Mark." We probably got in trouble at one point for the graffiti but, if so, I've blocked it out; at any rate, it's water under the bridge now.

When there was no traffic, we would race! And go to Kristi's house to see the chickens! And Holly's farm to watch her daring brothers fight with BB guns! And my cousin's place to see if my aunt made cookies! And follow a circuitous route to pet everyone's barn dogs and cats, sing songs into the next township, catch glimpses of wildlife, spy through open curtains, and generally procrastinate just a bit more on our 4-H projects.

Twilight was better-be-home time. If the dust-suspended air was tinged pink, then the landscape was sure to be accompanied by flashlights or headlights—our parents or relatives or neighbors enforcing curfew and reinforcing how much they worried. And how much they loved us.

I wish I could remember learning how to ride. I know Dad taught me. Mom would have been perfectly happy to help, of course, but she was busy sewing or grading papers. Now Dad is no longer in this sphere to ask. I guess he taught me so well it feels like I've always just known how. There is a vague recollection of training wheels . . . but it may have had something to do with taunting the little brother while he was in that phase. (I could be a tad mean in youth . . . but let's circumvent those details.) I'm sure for the first few yards without the trainers, I was worried and wanted Dad to hold on to my hand. But I'm equally sure I wanted to let go and do it "all by myself."

One infamous evening, my Peloton playmates couldn't join me, so I rode solo. I'm not a daredevil, but for whatever reason (ahem: immaturity), I decided to show off some Look-No-Hands skills while passing Dad in his Deutz in the adjacent field. He was pulling a cultivator and I was pulling a stunt . . . a.k.a. faceplant, that sent me, bleeding and dirty, home to Mom and a series of cold, dark washcloths ("warsh" cloths, if you prefer).

But it didn't scar me for life. Okay, fine—literally it did. There's a crooked scar on my knee, but it is in good company with many others, on many other freckled spots. Those just go to show I didn't let the incident—or much—slow me down. I guess the "what doesn't kill you" so-called truism was actually true in that instance. (But IMHO it's generally a load of [insert your favorite farm animal "gifts" here] in many others.)

Of course, Dad had been concerned while witnessing my solitary smash-up, but not in a position to be of immediate help. Close, yet too far. He had been about to shut down the tractor when he finally saw me bounce back up (er, rather, roll and stumble) and start walking (er, rather, using the bike as a crutch while limping back to the farmhouse), so he knew I would be OK.

That instance, I would imagine, was a microcosm of Mom and Dad's parenting. Try to equip us kids with a few tools, some basic skills, and hopefully some critical thinking. Then let go of our hands and observe from a distance . . . no matter how many tiny little heart attacks.

Because there would never be a time when worries didn't present themselves, at least as statistical probabilities. If a thing had wheels, chances are it was like a magnet for us kids. Roller skates: oh, the skating parties, with the best music and cute deejay and backwards skating sessions temporarily clearing the floor of some competition! A little red wagon: naturally; no farmstead is complete without one. Riding mowers: did I mention singing into the next township?! (The roar of the little engine didn't cover the crooning as much as I thought it would.) Pickup trucks: Dad's was so rusty there was a hole in the floorboard—or was that Uncle John's? Minivan: this was merely tolerated, when it was the only choice, but I had my license and was going to use it, by golly. Tractors: I was allowed to drive the Deutz, too, making my cousins jealous—haha! Then, post-farm, roller blades: a whole college campus-worth of sidewalks practically all to myself on warm and sleepless nights (I hated parties and I rarely observed the ritual of all-nighter study sessions). Skateboards: okay, that lasted about two seconds as I was reminded my middle name was not "Grace." And even a motorcycle: until I decided I enjoyed the roll bars and other safety features of my enclosed vehicle; not to mention the surround-sound stereo, climate control, cupholders, and lots of space for stuff. Evidently adulthood can do that to a person.

I wish I could say my fearless enthusiasm stayed with me while "adulting." It did for a while, particularly for a few glorious years when I lived in Riverside, Wichita, Kansas, Good Ol' US-of-A, Planet Earth, Solar System, et cetera, round-and-round. This was before Bike Walk Wichita was born, and cycle/stroll-friendly paths were limited to the river's edge. At least, the ones I knew about (this was before worldwidewebz addictions, too). It was one of the more tolerable forms of exercise, and an aspect of joyriding remained . . . at least for those of us who are easily enchanted by changes in the weather, the seasons, the river. But then, one day when I wanted to ride my bike, it was just gone. It had been stolen out of the garage which my well-meaning landlady hadn't yet put a door on, so was more of a glorified car port. I could have kept my bike inside my tiny half of the duplex—and I did sometimes—but mostly I was a trusting soul and didn't worry too much about it. And evidently someone needed it more than I, so . . . well, just so. I had other means of mobility. Then I married into Park City, whose name sounds promising, but is currently a colorless void on KDOT's Kansas Bicycle Map.

I'll circle back to it eventually, I swear. I have another bike, one with removable wheels for easy trunk transporting to preferred cycling locales. And a friend who is a fairly new cycling enthusiast, so I could likely keep up my pace if I felt I needed a buddy (adult translation: accountability partner). And I am aware that opportunities for resolutions and new beginnings come around all the time.

At least, as often as there are sunrises and sunsets.

DK/UNBOUND 2016, photo by Dave Leiker

DK/UNBOUND 2017, photo by Dave Leiker

DK/UNBOUND 2016, photo by Dave Leiker

DK/UNBOUND 2017, photo by Dave Leiker

Kristi Mohn:
Life Time Marketing Director,
UNBOUND Gravel Instigator and Organizer,
and Woman on a Bike

105 Meadowlark Reader Interview

Tim Mohn and Kristi Mohn

Kristi Mohn might be described as a typical Kansan. She was born and raised in Emporia by parents who were also born and raised in and near Emporia. Her mother was a stay-at-home mom, pausing her teaching degree while raising children, until Kristi entered high school. Her mother went to high school too, as an Emporia High School English teacher and journalism instructor. "Mortifying," Kristi says, the smile on her face making it clear that she somehow survived. Kristi's dad was a veterinarian. Pillars of the community. The whole family.

Like so many of us born and raised in Kansas, the desire to get away was strong. "In high school, I was probably at the top of the list of students who would most likely leave Kansas." And leave she did. Kristi attended the University of Kansas, studying Spanish and Education Curriculum and Instruction. Post college she made her way to

California, Costa Rica, and eventually back "home" to Emporia. Kristi and her husband, Tim Mohn, bought Flint Hills Music store. The couple settled into Emporia to raise their twins surrounded by family. Kristi began teaching at Emporia State University and joined her sister Beth in a real estate career.

"My dad and I were upstairs finishing the floors at Flint Hills Music, and I was saying to him, 'You need to do this, and you need to do that,' and telling him what he needed to be doing as an adult society member of this community. He stood up and said, 'Who is this you? Why me? What about you? You need to be doing this. This is your hometown. This is where you're from, and you live here now, and you have kids. *You* need to be doing this.'"

It was a moment for Kristi, "that moment where you go from being a kid to an adult." From there, Kristi joined the Emporia Arts Council Board and had the experience of being a member of the team that restored the Granada Theatre. She then became involved in the Chamber's Building Futures group.

Members were asking the question: What types of events could we bring to Emporia? "I literally thought, we don't need to bring new events. We need to look at existing events and see if the people who have those passion projects have any interest in expanding, growing, marketing . . . let's pick the people who are already doing the work and have a good foundation."

In 2006, Tim was one of two Emporians who participated in a 200-mile gravel bike race, the first DK/UNBOUND Gravel event. That race had thirty-four participants and had gained a bit of a following (approximately 200 participants by 2010). Biking on the gravel roads around Emporia had become a "date activity" for Kristi and Tim. They often rode their bicycles early mornings. Kristi jokes that when she would call to hire a babysitter, they always had to clarify if they needed the help AM or PM. As it was already a bit of a passion project for her family, she sat down with the founders of the gravel bike race, Jim Cummins and Joel Dyke. She told them she'd like to grow the event. She wanted to know what their thoughts were, and they were amenable.

And the rest is . . . a story of a lot of work and sweat and planning resulting in a community that is now known worldwide as a gravel biking destination.

We sat down to talk to Kristi about bikes and the community of Emporia on the day before registration for the 2022 event was to close. Kristi was expecting around 4,000 riders, 400 or so locals, across all race distances. The multi-day event now hosts ride lengths of 25, 50, 100, 200, and 350 miles, and a Juniors race. Today Kristi's title is Marketing Manager for Life Time, the company that bought the event in 2018. She works with managers of all thirty-three Life Time events with a focus on diversity, equity, and inclusion planning. Her job is to give access to under-represented groups at event start lines.

Kristi's focus is the off-road events, mostly biking, and she remains a key figure in the on-the-ground running, planning, and operations of UNBOUND Gravel, which takes place each year the first weekend after Memorial Day. She doesn't like to talk about this part, but if you Google gravel bike races, her name tends to come up. (She's kind of a rock star in the gravel biking world, but we will refrain from calling her that.)

One side effect of hosting the world's largest gravel bike race is that quite a few Emporians have become bike enthusiasts. Through the summer months there are at least four to five social group rides taking place each week. Kristi has been a part of that movement. She's been riding, as well as hands-on helping to grow the event. And one thing that Kristi noticed from the beginning was that she was often the only woman out there. Especially at the race starting line.

"This is always such an emotional one for me, honestly, really trying to understand why we weren't seeing more women at our start line. There was a piece of it, as we were looking at it and working through it, that I begin to understand. We needed to do two things. We needed to give women permission, and we also needed to invite them. They needed to know that they had a place and that it was okay to choose themselves."

Prior to 2017, about 9% of the race participants were women. Kristi wanted to see that change. "Men never have a problem signing up. They don't have to ask if it's okay if they spend X amount of dollars, X amount of time on themselves. They just assume that they can do it. And, of course, I'm speaking very globally, in generalizations. But even with Tim, who is an amazing supporter, he never asked when we had two young kids. If he wanted to sign up for a race, he signed up for a race and told me about it later. Where what I would do is, I would think: How am I going to deal with the training and with the kids? And I'd ask him if it was okay."

For the record, Tim would say yes.

"I felt like gravel, and the event itself, provided an opportunity. It was the perfect platform to tell women, 'You can ride 200 miles, and you can take the time to do the training. It's okay. You are welcome. And we want you here.'"

With the rest of the team on board, the "200 women, 200 miles" campaign began. They set a goal of 20% female participation in the race in three years. Registration opened, and they met that goal in three hours. "I felt very validated . . . All of the beliefs that I had come to hold about how women—how we rank ourselves really, in our own personal situations—the studies showed they were true."

"Choose yourself," is Kristi's message to women. "We've been taught to put everyone else's needs before our own, but sometimes you just have to choose yourself first.

"Currently we see a participation of around 32% female. In the 25 [mile race] it's actually over 50%. I really do hope that women feel comfortable signing up for that 200 if they want to, but also understand that we still bear the brunt of the family responsibilities and training for 200 miles isn't an easy task. It takes a lot of time. Choosing the 100, or the 25, or whatever. If it fits in your lifestyle, it's where we want you to be. I'm super proud of our women's percentages. It's higher than almost any other gravel event.

"It's interesting because it hasn't gone away. There's a part of me that thinks, 'Okay, we've been there, done that, so now we can move on to something else.' No. We're still doing that campaign. It was launched in

2016 for the 2017 event, so it's still relatively new, and when we watch these registrations, it's still relevant . . . You continually see the inequality and—although, I never have a problem signing up for events, and I've talked to other women who kind of fall in that vein—we also understand that those initiatives giving women permission and asking them to join can't stop yet because we are nowhere close to it being an equal playing field."

Kristi's initial foray into the world of gravel bike racing was as an economic driver for her community. Has she succeeded? One marker would be to look at the number of restaurants in downtown Emporia today versus twelve years ago, when the local farmers market got involved in the event as a way to help event organizers feed the 200 racers and company that would be in town for the event. A crew of volunteers served pasta with homegrown market sauce sourced directly from the vendor gardens. Today Emporia's downtown features a popular brewery, a Vietnamese restaurant, a Midwest American bistro, a popular Mexican restaurant in a now-larger location, and more. Some might say that the mood of the city seems to have changed. Downtown Emporia seems abuzz with activity, even through these cold winter months. Buildings are being refurbished, and new buildings have been built. An incubator space at the Emporia Main Street office has launched its first protégé, with plans being made for more. *Choose Emporia*, so many citizens seem to be saying. *We can do this. We can put ourselves first.*

Kristi Mohn will always be on a bike. "That's my happy spot, for sure. UNBOUND Gravel surpassed my expectations probably four or five years ago. I remember an interview I had with [KVOE radio legend] Ron Thomas at the civic [auditorium] after an awards ceremony breakfast. He was like, 'Are you surprised by this?' And I said, 'No, I always thought we could do this.' But now . . . It's outrunning me at this point."

In 2021, after a break year in 2020 for the COVID-19 pandemic, the race was live-streamed by FloSports and the response was enormous.

"We were hearing reports that the [professional bike] athletes that were doing the Tour [de France] were centering their training around watching our event in Emporia. Like, what? This is Emporia, Kansas! This is my hometown. How did we get this? How did we get to be the place athletes journey back to every year?

"We are a destination. I think that's a really cool concept . . . to think about the town that I couldn't wait to leave, it has become the town that my kids don't want to leave. How did that happen? That's a big change in a lifetime. It's pretty cool."

UNBOUND Gravel, née DK
by Julie Johnson

I spy the narrow crescent of the moon as I drive east on Sixth Avenue, eagerly anticipating the start of the 2021 edition of UNBOUND Gravel. Not that I would be riding. No, I merely want to experience the energy as around 2,000 bikers, supported by their friends and family, begin a long day of pedaling on gravel through the Flint Hills of Kansas.

For the 6:00 AM start of the 200-mile race, riders line up behind signs indicating their anticipated hours to finish—8 hours, 12 hours, etc. Vehicles from the sheriff's department, police department, and ESU campus police are in front, ready to lead the riders north on Commercial Street, jog west to Merchant Street, and out of town to the gravel. Standing at the corner of Twelfth and Commercial affords a spectacular view of the waves of bicyclists streaming by. It seems there is no end to the cyclists, but, finally, the last of the 1,002 makes the turn to head out of town.

An hour later, the 100-mile group follows a similar plan. As I head home, I hope for some cloud cover to protect the riders from the hot Kansas sun. Several times during the day, as I go about my chores, I remind myself that the riders are still out there on those bicycle seats, pedaling.

The whole week affords the opportunity to talk to visitors, Emporians, and, sometimes, a surprise encounter. Thursday afternoon as a friend and I enjoyed latté outside a downtown coffee shop, we talked about events of the coming weekend. Friday at 3:00 PM, 110 riders would start out on the 350XL. When I said that I intended to come down to see the start, she said, "What kind of people climb on a bike to ride 350 miles on gravel? Text me a photo."

As I did that, I commented, "They all look fairly normal to me."

While waiting for the start, I saw a familiar, though unexpected face. Sporting typical biking clothing and a face dripping with sweat, a daughter of a long-time friend was enjoying an ice cream cone. Although she hasn't lived in Emporia for many years, she had journeyed from Kansas City to Emporia to ride and had just finished the 25-mile race. She was waiting for her daughter, who was riding in the 50, to arrive.

The Finish Line Party hosted by Emporia Main Street starts early on Saturday and ends late. The chute down the middle of Commercial Street provides a lane to the race finish line. People line up on the street to ring cowbells, high five, and cheer the cyclists, welcoming them as they come back into town. Names of riders are announced as they arrive at the finish. Booths in the Expo highlight bicycles, clothing, nutritional items, and anything biking-related. Food trucks offer a variety of options—bar-b-que, tacos, pasta, Asian noodle bowls, and cinnamon rolls. Freshly squeezed lemonade quenches many a thirst on this warm, sunny day. Free State Brewery in Lawrence has even developed a special beer for the event. Unbound, a Kölsch beer is also a tasty refreshment.

Standing along the chute, I begin talking to a young couple. She went to school at ESU, got a job in Texas, met and married her husband, and talked him into moving back to Kansas City. "What brings you to the race?" I ask. He has come to cheer on a college friend who now lives in South Carolina and is riding in the 100. A little later I strike up a conversation with a couple from Palm Gardens, Florida. They are on vacation, heard about the race, and decided to stop and check it out. They had their bicycles with them, so after all the official riders had left, they went out to ride on the course.

When it's time for dinner, we go to check out the food trucks. While enjoying my fish taco, I visit with a couple from Duluth, Minnesota, here for the seventh time. He was here the year of the mud. Today they only rode the 100. He says that one of the things that sets UNBOUND

Gravel apart from other races is the buy-in by and the friendliness of the community. In fact, that is a comment I hear often from participants in this event.

After dinner we go back to the chute. Across from us stand retired ESU colleagues proudly displaying their tag indicating that they had finished the 25-mile ride on a tandem bicycle. A stroll past the finish line has riders eating, drinking, walking, and resting. Some have changed out of their cycling clothes, and I chuckle when I look at their legs—tan from mid-thigh to ankle, white the rest of the leg.

As we head home, well before the last riders arrive at 3:00 AM, I realize what a joy it has been to savor the excitement of gravel-grinding again this year. The logistics and planning necessary for such an event boggle my mind. What began in 2006 as the Dirty Kanza, a one-day race for thirty-four bicyclists starting in a motel parking lot, has evolved into UNBOUND Gravel, a weeklong event attracting thousands. Special people with a vision, others whom they have recruited to help, and many volunteers have created an event that the whole community can be proud of.

Dust on My Shoulders: A Flint Hills Gravel Story
by Kerry Moyer

The rider was standing there, dusty arms draped over bars, leaning over a dusty bike, dusty Hawaiian print shirt hanging on a tall frame, like some scarecrow on the side of a rough rock road under a scorching Kansas sun.

I slowed my bike and rolled toward this guy who looked "in trouble" and asked him if he was all right. My friend, Casey, who's ridden with me for years, asked the guy the same question, and we waited for an answer. The rider raised his head, looked at me, then Casey, with glassy eyes. He looked down, shook his head, looked up again and said, "I'm out of water. Do you have any water?"

I looked at his bike and checked out his setup and saw two bottles in two bottle cages. I glanced at Casey who saw the same thing I did. The math for a gravel grind, the amount of fluid needed for a hot and humid day, is no less than one 24-ounce bottle for every ten miles, and maybe more if you are climbing a lot of hills or if the heat and humidity is really high. The water you are drinking will need salt and sugar in it—electrolytes—for energy and hydration so you don't bonk or cramp. Cramps are hell and "bonking" is when there is nothing left in you. This can lead to ketoacidosis, and it is very dangerous. Riders need to stay hydrated. If you get dehydrated enough, you can't piss, your blood pressure goes up, and you can get really sick, even die. Heat exhaustion is no joke, and heat stroke is deadly.

Fact: Eating and drinking will keep you pedaling and keep you from needing an IV, or worse.

I didn't think Hawaiian shirt guy did his math.

We were twenty-eight miles into a 104-mile gravel grind on a rutted dirt road in the middle of nowhere, chunks of limestone every couple of inches, and it was hot. We had this guy on the side of the road, in bad shape, twenty-six miles from the halfway point and needing water. Casey and I both knew the score. This fella in his festive Hawaiian shirt with his two bottles, when he needed at least three more, was in over his head, and I'd guess he wasn't the only one assessing his life choices at that moment. Every fifty yards or so, there were riders out of their lines (the best path forward, where you try to keep your tires so you are less likely to get a flat or wreck in rough stuff) and on the side of the road, hanging on their bikes, trying to find the will to keep moving toward the halfway point, Council Grove, Kansas, for UNBOUND Gravel 2021.

I asked Hawaiian shirt guy his name. With a thick southern drawl, the rider introduced himself as Ben and told us he was from Alabama. I offered Ben from Alabama a bottle, and he took it, said, "Thank you," and opened it to take a drink. Giving Ben my bottle was going to make it tough going. It would put me at one-and-a half bottles, not quite enough to get to the halfway point in Council Grove, but this wasn't my first long gravel ride, and I saw a rider in need. Casey and I introduced ourselves and took a moment to rest. Ben shared that he was an accountant and wanted to try a 100-mile gravel event. He wanted to ride UNBOUND Gravel, here in these Flint Hills. Ben from Alabama told us that he was coming to realize that he would not finish, but he was still glad he'd come and called what he'd seen "beautiful." He told us that he had a heart condition and was not feeling very good. His face was red, and he was breathing heavy, and after a few seconds I said to him, "Hey man, no bicycle ride is worth your life."

Our newfound friend sighed and thanked me for my concern. He repeated what I said, "No ride is worth my life," and I realized he was looking through me. I thought, *He's not talking to me, he's talking to himself.* Ben then handed me one of his empties in trade for the water bottle I handed him moments before. He could have just poured the contents of mine into his, but he wanted a trade, I guess, or he was in a fog.

I'd been there, at my breaking point, my brain not working. I got to thinking this was part of his story now. Ben from Alabama told me that his name and phone number were on the bottle, and he said to me, "Go ahead and call to check on me when you get to the halfway point." I told him, in some earnestness, that he should probably have his SAG person, his support and gear person, come out onto the course to pick up him and his bike, or flag down one of the Jeep folks patrolling the course. I told him that he would need more water than I gave him, and it would probably be wise for him to call it a day. I told him I'd call him, although it felt like a strange request at the time.

Ben from Alabama told Casey and me that he wasn't quite ready to stop but would "go slow and play it safe." Ben did not seem to register that he was going to run out of water again before he got to Council Grove. He did not seem to appreciate that it was going to get hotter, stickier, and that the roads were only going to get more unforgiving. I knew, Casey knew, and every rider who had spent hard miles on these roads knew the score. Those last several miles before the asphalt of those Council Grove streets were not for Ben. He just didn't know it yet.

Before we left him, Casey offered Ben food. Ben, who was out of his element, out of his fitness level, out of his planning level, and at the mercy of the Kansas Flint Hills in early June, politely declined in his distinctive southern drawl.

The short rest from the stop helped Casey and me for a few miles, but the terrain, increasing heat, and thick humidity began making my own body start to fight me. Casey had fought cramps for miles, and our current predicament put Ben and his gravel story behind us while we kept moving.

COVID-19 had made training difficult, and neither Casey nor myself were as prepared for the ride as we had hoped. To add to our difficulties, Kansas and its unpredictable weather had given us a cold spring and only one week of heat and humidity to prepare and acclimate to these conditions. The heat was an increasing factor. We had to hunker down in the proverbial "pain cave" and find our will, watch our hydration and our food intake, and try to get to the halfway mark for rest, more hydration, food, and a tune-up for our dusty bikes.

At around mile thirty-seven, Casey's legs locked up at the top of a hill. Cramps are a painful time killer, but they passed, and we kept pedaling. We picked a more manageable pace. We hadn't figured Ben from Alabama or Casey's cramps into our math for the day. At around mile forty, Casey cramped again. I could see the pain written on his face, and he couldn't so much as lift a leg to get off his bike to stretch. Casey told me right then that he couldn't make the cutoff. We had started around sunrise and needed to be in Council Grove by a set time or we were done. We stood there, leaning against our bikes, contemplating our increasingly less negotiable situation when an old gravel friend, John, rolled up on us. Casey told me to go on, and he'd ride into Council Grove with John, so I clipped back onto my bike and mashed like hell to get those last hard miles to the halfway point. The whole time I wondered if leaving Casey was the right thing, but I was hungry to get to the finish line, and John was willing to roll with Casey in my place.

Council Grove would provide a much-needed oasis before heading toward Lake Kahola and the very long, steep climb known as the Kahola Crusher. After that climb, it would be an easier road en route to the glorious chute. Two years earlier, I'd climbed that hill on my way to the chute, the cheers and cow bells clanging for my third Dirty Kanza 100 finish in the books. This UNBOUND 2021 would be different.

I had been riding alone for some time, and I had felt the twinge of cramps after having gone through a very rough section of road that had body-breaking, bike-breaking rocks and ruts that stopped momentum, a road where I saw at least two riders lose their will and pull their cell phones from dusty jersey pockets. One of them was a woman from Missouri whom I'd met along the way. Shortly after wishing her well, I nearly went down when my front tire glanced off a big, sharp limestone rock, smack dab in the middle of my line while going a little too quickly down a chunky hill. A crash likely would have landed me in the ER. By now I knew my situation. The clock wasn't forgiving, and the math just wasn't looking promising. I had run out of water at mile forty-eight and was thirsty, my lips and throat dry. In our easy lives, we forget about how much we need water, how we are made up of so much water, and how heat and exertion will shrivel us up, turn us into dry, dusty husks. I pushed through some minor cramping and finally saw the nature trail entrance, but it didn't matter. I had zero minutes to go five miles. The clock had run out on my UNBOUND 2021. The math and circumstances beat my plan, Casey's plan, and Ben from Alabama's plan.

I coasted into Council Grove. People lined the road, cheering and clapping. Not one of them knew my ride was over. I didn't look directly at anyone, lost in second-guessing, the realization that I wouldn't be able to continue. Their cheers pushed me further into my acute sense of failure.

Hanging on my handlebars like some scarecrow—dusty, thirsty, tired, and having failed to reach the midpoint on time, I accepted a cold water bottle from a friend. I was second guessing everything. My friend offered support, said I still had fifty-four hard miles to go, but I was still out there, in my head, wanting to stay on the gravel and find that finish line again. Looking down, I saw the empty bottle with Ben from Alabama's name and number on it and wondered where he was on his road, whether he was still pedaling and found a way, or if he dialed someone and called it a day. I wondered if his story would have Casey and me lending him a hand. I wondered if Ben got the life-affirming adventure he was looking for and if he'd share his gritty gravel story with colleagues in the clean confines of a boardroom, with friends at the local pub over a beer, at the dinner table with his family. I wondered if he'd come back and try again.

I'd lost a friend two years prior during the same event, from a heart attack at the top of D hill, eight miles into DK 2017. In that moment of reflection, I remembered Ben's simple request.

With a somewhat shaky hand, I entered Ben's number into my dusty iPhone and hit send. Ben answered with his warm southern drawl, and we closed our gravel story with words of thanks. Ben from Alabama, Ben who came for an adventure, is now part of my gravel memories, as sure as the dust that settled on my shoulders on that hard June day under a scorching Kansas sun.

DK/UNBOUND 2016, photo by Dave Leiker

DK/UNBOUND, photo by Dave Leiker

DK/UNBOUND 2017, photo by Dave Leiker

DK/UNBOUND 2015, photo by Dave Leiker

On Shaky Wheels
by Mary Kate Wilcox

My older sister flew as I meandered. Somehow, between growth spurts, our ages warped and reversed. Every year, she grew younger, even more full of lively exuberance as my inner self wrinkled. I puttered up and down the cracked sidewalk as my sister soared by, balancing miraculously on the seemingly enormous wheels of her bike. Tottering down the sidewalk on my training wheels, I enjoyed watching the robins pick fervently for earthworms in the grass lawn beside me or the squirrels bolting warily forward at strategic intervals to forage for crushed acorns in the road.

Perhaps due to my already wizened soul, I was relatively old when I learned to ride a real bike. I can't quite remember my age, but the first pictures of me I can find on a bicycle are from when I was eleven. Even more tellingly blank in my mind is the desire, or lack thereof. As a young child (maybe four or five), I found contentment on my training wheels, observing the world flashing by. Passing by my neighbor's rose bushes so slowly, so deliberately, I could count every coral-colored petal and keep pace with every bee. My sister's three years on me seemed insurmountable back then. Although we were both, even at that young, tender age, afflicted with spasms of anxiety, my older sister found a different way to cope. Whereas I dawdled along, momentarily safe in my minuscule bubble of tolerated risk, anticipating the horrors and ignoring the beauty of the wild world beyond, she leaned into the fear, charging headfirst into life, anticipating the consequences yet proceeding doggedly onward.

She rode her monstrous, terrifying bike down the road, a blur of red metal and hot skin all the way to the end of the block till forced to turn around and wait for her cowardly little sister. Often, I called her name desperately from my short tricycle. Although I was secure on the sidewalk, steady astride my chosen vessel, her rapidly dissolving shape filled my heart with dread. What if, just one time, she didn't turn around? And I was alone. Alone in the shadows of the dark houses lining my street, the nefarious figures of the neighbors daring to mow the lawn or take out the trash as I slunk down their sidewalks.

But she always returned, always executed the wild, teetering turn in the middle of the road, wheeling back to me with a familiar exasperation that alternately filled me with relief that my impending abandonment hadn't occurred or whirled my insides together into a steaming vat of guilt because I was constantly holding her back.

Eventually I grew to an age where training wheels were no longer socially acceptable. The extra set of wheels drew a line in my development that my loving, accepting parents would not cross. In trying to balance my future as a well-rounded, independent adult and shrouding my anxious mind, they chose the well-being of the future me. I can't say I blame them. My sweet, supportive parents, who so often told me to ignore the tirades and taunts of my school peers, gently scoffed at my terror in abandoning training wheels.

"You're a big girl now. Why do you need them?" my mother asked in an encouraging tone as we sat together in the living room, maybe trying to coax out a sense of dormant pride in me through all the layers of omnipresent self-doubt.

Instead, my mind vibrated with all the echoes of possibilities clanging against my skull. How could she not understand the fear clamoring within me? What if I fell? What if I broke a leg or even both legs? Wouldn't that make all our lives, specifically theirs, harder? And the even more terrifying possibility. What if I just couldn't do it? It would be years before I learned that not everyone's minds rattled like mine did, the toxic fluid of anxiety pulsing through my body in time with my very blood, my breath, my every moment of life.

My father's voice was even more gentle. He must have seen the terror in my face. "It's okay. We can help you learn."

My mother missed the fear, already absorbed in the pile of papers adorning her lap. As she viciously slashed through weak sentences and grammatical errors with her favorite blood red pen, her muttering voice could barely hide the familiar, exasperated scoff rising in her throat.

"When I learned, my parents took me to the top of the neighborhood hill and pushed."

I stared at her aghast from my usual perch on the green-carpeted floor, but she didn't look up again, already intent on a student's inadequacy. With a disgusted shake of her head, she sliced through another offensive sentence.

I could only imagine the possibilities. She would drag me to the top of that unending hill on Antioch. As the traffic roared by, horns blaring and music pumping in my skull, she would push. I could see four possibilities. Either I could fall quickly, preemptively throwing myself off the side of my sister's old, red bicycle, like a hero in an action movie hurtling from a burning building or an exploding car. But much more likely I would end up flopping onto the pavement like a gasping, dying fish, completely out of its element, enduring both pain and ridicule. Inevitably, the mother conjured by my anxious mind would get down on one knee to whisper insults in my ear. The entire pulse of traffic would screech to halt, rolling down their windows so I could hear the cackling within. No, this was an unendurable option.

There were two other options left to me then. I could let her push me and career wildly down the hill shrieking the entire time. Certainly, the front wheel of the bike would lurch into one of the long, deep cracks spanning the incline. And I would fly off the bike, slamming into the chain link fence lining a yard on the right of the sidewalk head first. The helmet would crack open like an egg. The irate owners would come barreling out of the house, screaming curses at my mother for my bloodying of their fence and the skull-shaped dent they would need to repair. And she would point to me and shrug, with slumped, defeated shoulders as if to say, "What do you expect?" We could wait for the ambulance and these figments of anxiety would all huddle around me, the furious homeowners and my somewhat amused mother, telling me to hang on, that I had to pay for the damages. I just couldn't die and leave this burden for them to take care of. And then the ambulance would be delayed due to the long, meandering gawk-block backing up Antioch all the way to the highway. And when the EMTs arrived, they would provide slow, reluctant care, joking together above my mangled body. I could practically hear their imagined voices ringing in my hypothetically crushed skull.

"Six years old and doesn't know how to ride a bike? Maybe she's better off."

My mother nodding emphatically in the background as I lose consciousness, never to wake again. A slow, painful, and expensive death most likely not covered by insurance. Because of course there must be a stipulation that by six the recipient must know how to ride a bike. If this basic skill is lacking, they are allowed to deny coverage and are also given permission to laugh about it. And on top of that, in cases of humiliating death, my parents now owe them money back.

I shook my head wildly, holding a trembling hand against my skull to check for cracks, trying to clear away the previous horrible option so the finale could unfold across my pulsing brain. The last option and the best. I would career down the hill calmly, allowing myself to scream internally in exchange for subtly bowing to the incontinence. My anxiety-conjured mother would cheer from above, weeping with joy that I had flown through this milestone so gracefully, so effortlessly, finally making her proud. And then, I would hit the gaping crack in the sidewalk, but fly left this time, my body hurtling into oncoming traffic. A quick, cheap death. The paramedics would assume I pissed my pants on the horrible impact (and who could be taunted for that), not during the far worse ascent. And my mother could tearfully give my eulogy, proclaiming that at least I died knowing how to ride a bike.

"Mary Kate, are you okay?" My dad's concerned voice broke through my imaginings. I must have been pale. Possibly he believed me to be sickly, maybe terminal, and wanted the insurance to cover my inevitable demise, so he took me up the street to learn how to ride a bike.

His approach was gentler. No hills, no traffic, and no sidewalks. He held me up as I clutched hard at the handlebars, peddling as slowly as possible over the smooth, deserted tennis court. But when he let me go, despite the absence of caverns, craters, and cackling strangers, I could not keep myself up. Each time, I slumped over, sprawling glumly over the cool clay below, wishing over and over that I could just stay there and watch the clouds chase each other across the sky, moving in ways I never could.

For a few years after that I stopped trying, paralyzed as I often was by fear. I could sort of say I could ride a bike as long as the questioner inquired no further into fundamentals such as balance. I forgot the feeling of a gusty breeze in my face, of keeping up with the leaves swirling and dancing across the neighborhood, imagining my training wheels would keep pace with the soaring resident red-tailed hawk.

For those intervening years, not riding a bike was easier than failure or the torment of using four wheels instead of two. But at eleven the agony of not riding a bike outweighed even those morbid imaginings. Unwittingly, stupidly, I revealed my cycling deficiency to a classmate. That year, everyone was riding bikes and to refrain became an unforgivable sin. Even though I lived far away from my peers and even though I had few friends, I began dreaming of riding bikes with them, maybe even beating them when we raced. Once again, I had found a panacea to all my childhood aches. Once again, the naive hope faltered and died, but at least I truly learned to ride a bike.

In some ways it was easier to learn as a gangly, awkward semi-teenager. I rode my sister's old bike despite the fact I had long ago shot up past her in height. Even though my knees clanged repeatedly against the handlebars, I felt safer. At least my long, bruised legs could reach the ground quickly at the slightest whiff of disaster.

But in so many ways my late learning was worse. My Dad helped me down the street, holding the metal frame until I could pedal my unwieldy self into balanced submission. I remember grinning with belated pride, only to have the rare smile drip off my face. Even though my father whooped with glee and my mother left her grading to watch my success, their happiness couldn't mask disdainful looks of the neighbors or the indignation of the recent infants wheeling by.

One day, taking a sharp turn very, very slowly (as was my style) I tipped over, unable to catch myself in time. I am still unsure if this fall was the result of my poor, newly developed biking skills or my anxiety. Across the street from that fateful corner stood a line of ramshackle houses. Tenants floated in and out through my childhood without names, constantly coming and going, leaving the houses in even more disrepair than the last.

At the time of my biking resurrection, it seemed that every house was occupied by throngs of teenage boys. I'm sure they had parents, but I never saw them. I only ever saw the boys. They often lounged in the garage of the middle-most house, smoking joints together in a loose circle or shooting hoops and cursing vehemently at each airball. That day, when I passed, they stopped their game to watch my slow progression down the sidewalk (I was still too scared to ride in the road).

The boys turned to face me in unison, six high school juniors formerly engaged in a furious game of three on three. Sweat dripped down the bare, pale chest of the boy in front and a large stud gleamed in his ear. With the ball tucked under one arm, he leaned over as another boy whispered in his ear. My face flushed with scarlet splotches. I stared down at the sidewalk, suddenly horribly aware of my mass of puffy brown hair piling up under the helmet like an untidy bird's nest, my legs encased in my favorite shorts, ugly green hand-me-downs from my father. My long, awkward, adult-sized body and elderly soul was bunched up on a child-sized bike. That experience alone would have been humiliating enough.

The boy in front slid his other, unoccupied hand into his pocket and drew out a phone. I glared back down at the pavement with tears glimmering in the corner of my eyes, every molecule within me hyper aware of the six sets of eyes trained on me and now the million sets of eyes possible through the camera of the phone. I told myself to concentrate. The sidewalk turned ahead of me, and I had to turn perfectly, without a wobble or lurch, without sticking my leg out to find reassurance against the ground. I stared down at the neat cracks fast approaching, at the unforgiving right angle of the turn. Suddenly in my mind, each crack was a chasm, the turn now life or death, and the boys beyond ravenous predators.

And I fell, almost comically slowly, thudding against the pavement with a dull thunk, too paralyzed to even pull myself off of the bike. I shut my eyes tight, hoping the infant strategy for hide and seek would work. That if I couldn't see them, they couldn't see me. Laughter erupted through my eardrums.

"Damn! That was better than I thought!"

"Dude, this'll get so many views!"

I curled myself up around the bike, wishing the cracks below me were actually deep ravines that I could fall into, landing anywhere but in this moment. A metallic squeaking began to break through the laughter, followed by the crunching of tires.

"Great." I thought. "They're coming to finish me off." The boys must have agreed on the best finale, the way to get the most likes. They would take turns running me over with their bikes, crushing me to death beneath the thick, rubber BMX wheels. There must be fancy bike tricks, wheelies and such, that look far more impressive when launching over and upon a corpse. I sighed, already resigned to my fate, my afterlife as a viral sensation.

A screech of brakes, a hand shaking my shoulder hard.

"Mary Kate, Mary Kate, are you okay?" My sister's voice, only that sound could wake me out of the shocked paralysis. Now fourteen, now streaked with a stubborn independence, my big sister no longer waited for me, an agreement struck when I finally learned how to ride a bike. She would go with me, accompany me for a bit at my agonizingly slug-like pace, and then hurtle ahead at a breakneck pace, glorying in the adrenalin of speed.

But, possibly not hearing me plod along behind, not shaking her head at me when I called her back to look at the birds or the blooming flowers, she careened around to find me lying here, attempting to dissolve back into the Earth.

I didn't answer for so long, she shook me again, harder this time.

"Mary Kate, are you okay? C'mon tell me."

My voice came out in an ashamed rasp. "Maggie, I fell. And they got me on video. Those boys. And they're going to post it." I swallowed back a sob.

I rocked back and forth trying to silence the whimpers now building up in the space behind my throat, concentrating so hard that I didn't notice her get up. Suddenly, the laughter died behind me and my eyes lurched up, terrified. This must mean something more ominous than glee. Maybe their video wasn't as funny as they hoped, and the blame lay solely with me.

But no, my sister, blazing with fury, years younger but just as tall, cornered the high school boys against their garage. She didn't need to shout. Her form looked oddly imposing, her head tilted forward and the helmet swinging from her hands as if she no longer needed it. When she charged them like a bull, they were the ones who would break.

Mutely, still sweating, the boy with the earring handed my sister his phone. He had shrunk back into his gangly form, no longer inflated by perverse amusement, just a skinny, pale boy who couldn't play basketball. She must have deleted the video because she tossed the phone back towards him. He flailed in the air, catching it at the very tips of the fingers. With a final look of disgusted derision, she turned away. Fury made her buoyant as she hauled me up easily, as if her righteous lightness was contagious.

We walk home together, our bikes squeaking beside us. The air begins to turn chilly, and a persistent breeze ruffles our clothes. I can see the red-tailed hawk wheeling far overhead, free and majestic and impervious. Exactly like my sister, exactly who I want to be. I can tell she itches to jump back on her steed and soar against the wind, but she waits, walking home with me in silence. My heart is swollen with pain and joy and love because again, as always, she refuses to abandon her anxious, nervous disaster of a sister.

In my pulsating, anxious brain, another image forms, my sister roaring along on her bike, and me, amazingly able to keep up, not buffeted by the wave of thoughts pounding over me, persevering through at last.

A Princess on a Bicycle
by Angel Edenburn

When I was a child, my parents lived in Salina, Kansas. I remember many hours spent on the back of my mom's bicycle. As a family, we only had one vehicle and my father needed it for work. Mom was happy when my father bolted the seat on her bicycle for me. It meant I didn't have to stay home when Mom went out shopping or on an adventure.

A few times a week, Mom would load me up and put me in one of those hard plastic seats bolted onto the back of her bicycle and buckle me in with the little black seatbelt and silver buckle. I was happy because we couldn't go as far and as fast if I had to ride in the little red wagon. Riding in the wagon was bumpy and not as much fun.

It was a short ride to the library. I loved it but had trouble using my inside voice and didn't like having to take the books back after I read them.

Sometimes, we would go for longer rides around town. It was disappointing there were no live Indians living at Indian Rock Park. That ride always made Momma tired because it was a long way almost straight up to the top of the hill. From there, we could see most of the town. But if I was lucky, Mom would ride all the way to the magical realm of Downtown.

I loved it when we went there. The plate glass windows in the shops along the street held so many wonderful things. New washing machines in colors of harvest gold and avocado green, big color television sets with remotes, all kinds of shoes, and pretty diamond and gold jewelry and watches. I loved riding by the department store the best. It had everything the other stores had and more.

Why was this my favorite? I loved seeing all the pretty dresses. I could do a magical thing called window shopping. Mom would slow down or stop and ask me which ones I liked. It was hard to decide. I got to choose what I liked from all of the dresses, not just the ones for little girls. When I finally made up my mind, I would tell her, and we would discuss the colors and designs on the ride back home.

I didn't know money was tight. I knew I had a mom who was amazing. She could sew! Like my grandma, her mom, Mom could make almost any frock, pinafore, or dress.

After I decided on the color and design I wanted, we would go home and plan. Mom would get out her stash of patterns and brown paper. A few days later, we might go across town. If we rode the bicycle, it meant The High Place. It was scary.

Mom had to get off the bicycle and walk it up the concrete ramp, over the road with traffic zooming below, and then back down the other side. Even though there was a cage around it, we were up so high, and I was scared until we rolled back onto the ground.

We would then ride for a few more blocks until we got to a different store, not like the ones downtown. Mom would park the bike out in front while we went inside. Depending on which store had the right fabric at the right price, we might have to go to Duckwall's, T G & Y, or Ben Franklin. Sometimes it took several days before we found the right fabric, thread, trim, and notions.

Mom's magic with patterns, sewing machine, and fabric took a few days. Sometimes I was lucky enough that I got clothes out of the leftover fabric from something Momma made for herself.

I loved riding on the back of the bike in the sunshine, with the breeze ruffling the white eyelet trim at the bottom of my dress. I felt like a fairy princess. All I needed was some gossamer wings, a noble tiara, and a sparkly wand. I pretended I had all of those things and more as we rode. Those days on the back of the bicycle were the happiest in my life.

The walkway is still there, but the stores are long gone. My love of window shopping, bicycles, and sewing remains. Sometimes, when I go back to Salina, I think of those magical days riding on the back of a bicycle.

Blue English Racer
By Debra Irsik

My dad owned Schwartz Bicycle Shop in Jetmore, Kansas, when I was growing up. Fixing everything from toasters to cash registers, he preferred to fix bicycles for people in our community. Dad would buy old bikes, overhaul them, paint them, and sell them from his shop. He had a Schwinn dealership for several years, but most of the bikes in the old-school bicycle stand in the shop were Western Flyer, Rollfast, or other bikes sold through Montgomery Ward or Sears catalogs. The Schwinn, considered an expensive bike, was not in my future unless he traded for one and fixed it up. Dad would usually order one or two Schwinns during the year, and they would sell as gifts for birthdays or Christmas. My siblings and I drooled over the new bikes, knowing they would never be ours.

My earliest memories are of Dad standing in the garage with axle grease on his hands and a bicycle frame in the bite of the big vice. He would tear them down and rebuild everything while chains soaked in something in a bucket to keep them lubricated. After re-building, they were like new.

Our family was His, Hers, and Theirs. Four children from Dad's marriage to my mother, my stepmother's son, whom my father adopted, and the two daughters my dad and stepmom had together. Feeding and clothing seven kids and two adults meant everyone had to compromise. Dad's job with the state highway department did not pay enough to make ends meet, so he also had a lot of side jobs and late nights. Our good-as-new wheels were only ours until someone wanted to buy them.

Then the miracle happened. Someone traded the bicycle of my dreams, a blue English Racer, for a new bike. I mooned over it, telling my father how well I would take care of it. Telling myself, "After all, the bike isn't new. It's a trade," I prayed every night that the slender, fine-boned beauty would be mine.

Most bicycles had a wide-tired and cumbersome appearance, but this one was the supermodel of bikes. She had narrow tires, three speeds, and was the color of summer sky. I could just imagine soaring down Park Hill with my hair flying behind me. It was my waking thought and the subject of my prayers at night. Finally, Dad said I could have it. I was in seventh heaven, over the moon. I loved the lightweight, sleek lines of this blue wonder. My brother warned me she would sail right out from under my happy bottom if someone bought her, but my joy-filled balloon did not pop.

I went rolling along until a girl at school got the same bike. We went to church together, and she told me she wanted her best friend, a missionary's daughter, to have a bike just like hers, and her father promised to purchase my bicycle. Devastated, I did not ask my dad if it was true. Surely, he wouldn't sell my bike knowing how much I loved it. Weeks passed, and he said nothing, so I buried my head in the clouds that follow young girls around.

The best friend was the daughter of missionaries who came back every summer and helped with Vacation Bible School. I loved the family. They were beautiful, kind people. I wanted to hate the girl, but I could not. She was one of the sweetest girls I have ever known, and I almost idolized her mother. I wished she were my best friend. I focused my anger on the girl that was a schoolmate. She was the traitor. She was the one trying to take my bike away.

Fortunately, God has a way of diffusing these little bombs or, as it played out for me, not so fortunately. My brother and I were riding home from school, and I'm sure he was prodding me to beat him. He had a banana-seated, re-furbished Sting-ray. It was what all the boys wanted so they could do wheelies and tricks and use up some of their abundant testosterone. I was doing my best to keep up, but no number of speeds could make up for the difference between my bird-legs and his boy legs. He was in front of me, taunting me to keep up when my lovely, skinny tires grabbed a pile of gravel and bucked me head-long over the handlebars and under the parked truck that I'd run into. Rick helped me up and somehow got me the rest of the way home. I had a deep gash flush with gravel and enough blood to convince him I was dying. My stepmom calmly cleaned the wound and declared that I would live to see another day. Unfortunately, the event opened the door for dad to decide the bike was too flimsy and unsafe. He gave me a sturdy replacement and sold my bike to the traitor's father.

I would see the girls almost every day on my way home. They were often riding the matching English Racers. I was heartbroken. I would rather walk than ride a different bike, but there was no way I would question Dad's authority, and it was over a mile to the school from our house, almost the opposite side of town.

The missionary kid was kind enough to tell me how much she appreciated the bike. She had already developed the ability to make a person feel valued. Convinced that my sacrifice was an act of kindness and grace, I made peace with her. I may or may not have carried a slight grudge against the schoolmate all the way through high school.

Blueboy

by Annabelle Corrick

The author in her bicycling era.

Blueboy never let me down. He went everywhere I wanted him to go, often beyond sidewalks and streets. He never had a wreck, never lost a race, or made me late to any place such as to school or home from school.

How could a girls bike be a "he"? Technically speaking, girls bikes are constructed for girls, it's true. You might ask Marilyn vos Savant, and someone did. Kayla liked the looks of a boys bike better. Marilyn replied that it's not just about the appearance of the lateral bar from seat to stem (pants vs. skirts). Girls and boys bikes "differ in ways that tend to suit each sex's body type." She cites girls' "shorter torsos and longer legs" that are accommodated by a narrower handle-bar width with shorter stem and a different seat construction on girls bikes.

But in the simple logic of my childhood, even though Blueboy had been constructed *for* a girl, that didn't mean he *was* one. Quite the contrary. In those days when Knighthood still had some semblance of being in flower, to my mind he had to be, of necessity, a strong cavalier. He was built very solidly with thickness of limbs (tires and handlebars) and stout overall construction as a knight should be. His bold, blue color could grace the face of any *Braveheart* warrior.

I didn't pick him out or request his type, color, or size. He merely appeared on schedule with my ninth birthday. Why the delay—the insistence on that rather advanced childhood age? In retrospect, I imagine the fate of William Allen White's daughter, Mary, on her last horseback ride might have left some fear in the hearts of parents of young girls about any kind of riding. Especially those who had lived in Emporia like my mother had.

Mary happily looked and felt as young as preadolescence while she was in her late teens. She defied contemporary conventions, wearing pigtails and exhibiting what her father called "a certain surplus energy" although he declared that the actual problem was "the limb of an overhanging tree." So at the outset of a vacation's horseback ride in my earlier childhood, my mother demanded of the rancher: "Give her a slow one!"

Yet I benefited from the younger kids next door who already had a pint-sized bike for easy training. I didn't have to wait to learn. They let me pedal in safety up and down their drive. My eldest bro's bike had fallen into disuse—a red and white vehicle that had seen better days and was too large for me anyway. Old Red and White originally transported our dad to work during World War II gas rationing. He and other war-time cyclists then resumed going to work via automobile. The resurgence of adult recreational biking was yet to come.

By the time I finally turned nine, eldest bro's basketball practice left him no time for bicycle riding. Two concrete slabs extended the single-car driveway, providing a shaded court amid the tall elms lining the street. An official-looking hoop appeared dead center over the garage door. Retrieving his free throws provided a teamwork experience of sorts, but when I was on Blueboy, the bike and I took off in a realm of our own, coordinated into a kind of technopathic, symbiotically-working duo.

Also around that time, my next-eldest bro received an upgrade from riding Old Red and White as a hand-me-down. He took well to his large English bike with skinny wheels, sleek design, and *three speeds.* To me that vehicle looked ominous—black with silver streaks, low handlebars, seat raised high and leather pouch behind. He disappeared for hours at a time on Big Black. If there had been an E. T. anywhere in or around town, he would have found it. For me and Blueboy, half an hour in the immediate area did just fine.

One day I joined him on an excursion. I don't recall why; I just know where—on the busiest streets towards downtown. In spite of his reassurance, "Just stay right behind me," apprehension gripped me. In my usual riding zone, I met pedestrians, other leisurely bikers, and only the occasional car. But now cars whizzed by in a steady stream. One careless swerve could be fatal. Fortunately, Blueboy didn't waver and miraculously kept up with Big Black. Topeka was no huge metropolis. Yet, I didn't experience anything so scary until I rode in a pedaled rickshaw through New York City's Times Square some decades later during a taxi strike.

Going beyond streets and sidewalks meant up and down driveways, down concrete steps, or down declines into steep ravines in Children's Park. Blueboy performed well on the various byways abounding in our neighborhood. The hazards hardly occurred to anyone. No children wore safety helmets, and young people comprised the whole of the cycling populace that I saw. If we were taking our lives in our hands, we remained blissfully unaware.

Some girls I knew in my preadolescent days craved horseback riding even though bicycles had become so prevalent. You didn't have to go far to find prairie land. They went crazy to have their own horse and *ride.* If I had gotten one, perched up so high on a galloping steed at thirty miles per hour; I might have hollered out a popular cry of the day: "Hi-ho, Silver and away!" Or if I was into speed and thrills, I might have craved a downhill-racer bike that could go almost twice that; but I did not.

Maybe I was missing something. It didn't seem like it. I had Blueboy.

One of the first girls bicycles.

1890s

Note on Bicycle Legalities:

After bicycles moved from indoor velocipede rinks to the outside, cities enacted restrictive ordinances. A book about the bicycle's influence on America reports that: "Early court cases regarding road use went against bikes—in 1881, three cyclists who very publicly defied a ban on riding in New York's Central Park were briefly jailed."

Progress for cyclists led to the 1890 landmark case *Swift v. City of Topeka* that "established bicycles as vehicles with the same road rights as any other conveyance." A cyclist riding on a vehicular portion of the bridge going over the Kansas River was convicted of violating an ordinance prohibiting bicycle riding on sidewalks and on the bridge. The Kansas Supreme Court reversed and remanded with instructions to dismiss the charges, stating that bicycles "are not an obstruction to, or an unreasonable use of the streets of a city, but rather a new and improved method of using the same."

By the turn of the next century, Topeka had wholeheartedly embraced biking as a municipal pastime. Special street lane markings and sign postings now designate bicycling routes throughout the city as part of the Shunga, Deer Creek, and Landon Trail network. Adult cycling groups and clubs often organize excursions and marathon trips. In the current milieu, a child riding about randomly is not the norm it once was.

Sidewalk regulations have relaxed a bit, but bicycles are still prohibited from sidewalks in the central business district. On the Shunga Bicycle/Pedestrian Trail, however, it is motor vehicles that are banned. While safety helmets are encouraged in Kansas, they are not required. Cyclists have formed their own advocacy groups and in 2011, the Kaw Valley Bicycle Club celebrated the passage of the Kansas 3-Foot Law regulating how cars may pass bicycles.

Sources:

Guroff, Margaret. *The Mechanical Horse: How the Bicycle Reshaped American Life.* Austin: University of Texas Press, 2016.

Kaw Valley Bicycle Club. "Kansas Bicycle Laws: Topeka's Traffic Regulations." *KVBC.org.* [Current]

"Swift v. City of Topeka," courtesy of our legal-eagle cycling friend Sarah E. *Forums.SegwayChat.org.* July 8, 2003.

"Then & Again." *The Washington Post Magazine.* December 8, 2002.

vos Savant, Marilyn. "Ask Marilyn." *Parade Magazine.* July 11, 2021.

White, William Allen. "Mary White." *The Emporia Gazette.* May 17, 1921, in Griffith, Sally Foreman, ed. *The Autobiography of William Allen White: Second Edition.* Lawrence, KS: University Press of Kansas, 1990.

WATERMARK
BOOKS & CAFE

WICHITA'S HOME FOR BOOKS SINCE 1977

Come & See Us!

OPEN

MON thru FRI **9 AM – 4 PM**

◆ *Thursdays* ◆

BOOKSTORE OPEN 'TIL 7PM

SAT and SUN **9 AM – 3 PM**

Shop online 24/7 at
WWW.WATERMARKBOOKS.COM

@WATERMARKBOOKS   @WATERMARKBOOKSANDCAFE   @WATERMARKBOOKS

A Green Bike

by Monica (Osgood) Graves

Christmas at our house was always a fun time. We didn't have much money, but Mom and Dad managed to get us gifts. Dad would go out to the pasture and bring home a small cedar tree for decorating. We gathered around with our homemade ornaments tied together with various colors of yarn, so many kids pushing and shoving for the best limbs to hang favored ornaments.

It was 1969, and I'd become a skinny, uncoordinated twelve-year-old. On that Christmas morning my siblings and I woke up to a big surprise, new bicycles across the floor and around the tree. My sisters laughed and latched onto their bikes while my brother hopped onto his bright red tricycle. I looked but didn't see one for me. Had there been a mistake? I gave my parents a puzzled "where's mine?" look. Dad grinned and pulled a large box wrapped in bright paper from behind the tree. He gave me a wink and spoke. "Here you go, Moni." I raised my eyebrows and looked at the package and then at Mom and Dad.

I plopped onto the floor and tore at the shiny paper. I was bewildered. My sisters looked on with astonishment, like I'd uncovered a chest full of treasure. Inside the box was a record player, a brand-new record player, a player of my very own. A record lay on the turntable ready to spin. I plugged it in, and the house filled with music. We listened to "All I Want for Christmas" and "I saw Mommy Kissing Santa Claus." Warm music on a cold day. Wow! Maybe my parents thought I wasn't ready for a bicycle. My frame was spindly and undeveloped. No matter. My parents knew I loved music. My gift wasn't a bicycle, but music was better.

Christmas Day was cold and snowy. My sibs couldn't ride bicycles on the country road, and it looked like it would be some time before they could go out and ride, but I could play music on Christmas Day. I could play music all day long and the following day, too, and so I did.

Spring came. I had shared my record player all winter. At least, I shared the music. As the weather warmed, we all spent more time outdoors. My sibs rode their bikes, and I wanted to ride, too. I expected them to share. After all, we had all enjoyed my music. They didn't agree with me.

"Nope, this bike is mine."

"There's a reason you got a record player."

"Wait until I get it broke in."

"Maybe later."

"After I finish, you can take a spin."

Okay. I got it. They had bicycles, and I didn't.

The sun shone, and the air was fresh. I went outside and saw the bikes parked near the porch, listing on their kickstands. They lured me. Connie's bike was forest green, decorated with a white stripe on each fender. It was beautiful. I decided to take it for a spin down the gravel road.

I hopped aboard and wobbled at first. Then I got my balance. Down the road I rolled. I reached a hill and went over the top and picked up speed. I realized that I needed to slow down. Oh, no. I did not know how to slow down. I needed help. I was alone. I'd ridden a single speed bike and knew how to use pedal brakes, but Connie's five-speed, green bike had levers on the handlebars, and I was at a loss. I was stumped, and I was picking up speed. I was flying down the hill, and I was scared!

Gravity took control the moment I lost it. I tumbled into the ditch, and my head bumped against a large rock. I lay still and got my breath and felt the bump with my fingertips. No blood. Okay. I was okay. I couldn't say the same for Connie's green bike. My injuries weren't serious, scraped knees, and a bump on the head, but the bike looked awful. The front wheel was bent, and much of the green paint was scraped off the back fender. I was sore, inside and out, but the bike was broken. I had to climb that hill with a wounded bike in tow. It was time to face the music. I feared my sister's wrath.

I walked into the house and found Mom in the kitchen. She turned and saw my scrapes and bruises and examined the bump on my head. I answered her, "What happened to you?" with my story and nodded when she said, "You're lucky you weren't hurt too bad."

I don't recall the details, but Dad repaired the bike. I know I was not allowed to ride Connie's green bike again. That was fine with me. She was upset, and I didn't blame her. When I wanted to travel, to get to the creek or go down the road, I saddled a horse or walked. When I stayed home, I listened to my music or read a book. I had all I needed. I didn't need a bike.

Annual Convention — October 2022
www.KansasAuthorsClub.org

A Rare Find
by Alexander Hurla

There it lay. Without being overly dramatic and saying that the sight stopped me in my tracks, I will say that my pace slowed as I studied the object in front of me.

What I'm looking at is not one of the countless Link electric scooters that block sidewalks and occasionally wind up in trees after college students' late-night escapades. No, this mode of transportation, with its bright Granny Smith-colored frame and no-fee riding, is one of the legendary Green Apple Bikes of Manhattan, Kansas.

I've never seen one in the wild like this. My few glimpses of the rare bikes were of ones already domesticated, ridden between the legs of their keepers. This one is laying halfway on the crumbling asphalt of the alley behind our house so that some careless driver might put it out of commission. As I move toward the bike, I glance around for anybody coming to retrieve it. Perhaps it does have a temporary owner who dropped it off momentarily. I'm having a hard time believing this could be real after living in Manhattan for nearly five months and never finding one of these bikes.

There is no one around. Yet, I have a feeling that someone might walk out of any of these houses on either side of the alley to reclaim the bike they've left behind. I inch closer, my gaze shifting between the bike and the houses.

I'm now just a few steps away. I know that if I mean to take this bike as my own, I need to move quickly. Without thinking, I grab the bike by the handlebars, stand it up, and hop on. My ears are alert and listening for a shout or yell, someone telling me they've only left the bike for a moment, and they want it back. I push down on the pedal and shoot forward. I don't hear anyone as I turn onto the street.

I quickly realize there are no brake levers on the handles. Instead, I discover, the brakes engage when peddling backwards, and I stop doing this after the first lurch forward from the bike's abrupt stop. The front fender is also a different shade of bright green than the frame and looks like it's been salvaged from some other less fortunate machine. It rattles every time I hit a bump.

There are cars parked on either side of the street, and a college student clad in a K-State sweater is walking his dog who wants to sniff every blade of grass and fallen twig. My eyes drift over to see if the man is mesmerized by the bright green bike streaking passed him. I can't tell what his reaction is as I turn left towards campus.

With each pedal I feel joy coming over me. Just as any town has a list of things to see and do in order to say that you've truly been there, Manhattan boasts a diverse array of experiences. From ordering a grilled mac and cheese sandwich from the Varsity Food Truck in Aggieville at 1:00 AM to walking up the hill to the "Manhattan" sign, there is a long list of things you need to complete before saying you've been to the city. One of the most difficult boxes to check is exactly what I'm doing right now because of how well these bikes hide.

After considering how special riding this bike is, and some half-hearted attempts to pop a wheelie, I get the idea to ride over to my brother's apartment and show off my prize. I know he'll be impressed at seeing one of these bikes.

I pull up next to his front door. My legs feel like jelly, and I realize it's been months since I've ridden a bike. I shake them out and call my brother.

"Hey, come check out my new ride," I say as soon as he answers. I can tell his mind is racing, trying to figure out what I mean. Plus, it's the early afternoon, so he's probably just woken up. He may have been on one of those late-night escapades that cause Link scooters to end up in trees. I'll have him answer that once he reads this story.

"Are you outside?" he responds after a moment.

"Yeah. Come see this speed demon," I say, only partially sarcastically. I bet he would appreciate taking a ride on it since he's never been on one before.

I roll the bike closer to his door so he can see it as soon as he comes out. I'm excited the thought of how shocked he will be.

The door opens, and he laughs as soon as he sees the bike. "Where'd you find that?"

With great satisfaction, I relay my tale of adventure, almost feeling like a celebrated explorer or a knight of old. In the middle of my saga, somebody walks up from the parking lot.

"You giving that away, Ty?" the guys asks my brother.

I stop my account. Now I'm the one trying to figure out what something means.

"No, he found this one," Ty says, and the guy gives me an approving nod before he goes inside.

"What did he mean about you giving this away?" I ask.

"Oh. I've got one in the living room."

It takes me a moment to process this. I look down at my bike. It looks less bright than I thought it did before. I notice some scratches on it, and the fender seems to rattle all the time now.

"Yeah," he says. "I've been trying to get rid of it for weeks."

It starts to sink in that perhaps my exploit is not as thrilling as I initially thought. Maybe everyone in Manhattan has ridden one of these except me. Maybe I'm just a terrible finder. The more I think about it, the more I think that might be the case. Yet, I finally have my trophy and intend to get a little more fun out of it.

"You want to take a ride?" I ask. "We could be the Green Apple Bike Gang."

He's used to my corny jokes and agrees. We cruise down Aggieville and through campus before releasing the bikes back into the wild for someone else to have their own adventure and, if they're as bad at finding these bikes as I am, check off the box of riding a "rare" Green Apple Bike.

The Wind Did Not Rush That Day
by Lisa Allen

There are two bikes rusting in my backyard, both chained under the nail-popped deck, behind the makeshift shelf that holds charcoal for the red Weber grill my dad's friend, Don, gave him that he then gave to me. Three bikes, if you count the little green bike my second son rode exactly one time before declaring it stupid. Four, if you count the pink princess bike that has since lost its seat, the bike my youngest wanted when they used the pronoun *she* and wore purple ribboned pigtails to school.

The two bikes I'm thinking of cost me a tax refund. My youngest and I bought them at Walmart. We were late to the game, so there were only a few from which to choose, but that didn't keep us from spending an hour comparing colors and styles and prices. It took another good half hour to wedge them into my Chevy Lumina—one in the trunk, the other angled diagonally from the backseat to the front—and another hour to make the fifteen-minute drive home. I had to stop every ten minutes to re-wedge. I was terrified the one in the trunk would fall out, that the car behind us would mangle its frame unusable, that our plans of afternoon rides would give way to insurance claims or an accident or two bikes we'd keep chained up but never use.

I had not ridden a bike since high school. Then, in my little Kansas town, I'd climb on after work, when it was dark, and fly down the streets with my hands at my sides. It was the rush of air I craved after a waitressing shift, the quiet that never came in a house with five siblings. I loved the wide-open streets, loved that the only noise was crickets.

Maybe an occasional car. I'd pedal past classmates' houses, peek inside their open-curtained living rooms, their lives backlit in unforgiving fluorescence and 90-watt bulbs. So many recliners, just like ours. TVs too, imposing against a far wall. I imagined their shag carpeting, their closed bedroom doors, the holes in the walls their fathers surely put there, too.

Helmets weren't a thing when I rode. Or if they were, they weren't a thing in our home, in my town. Memory is funny that way, picking and choosing what it keeps readily available. I don't remember who first taught me to pedal without training wheels, nor do I remember a first bike or a second or a third. What I remember is the ten-speed I took to when I needed space, something other than chicken grease or cigarette smoke in the air that blew my hair. The ten-speed I parked in the garage of the house we moved into after my dad married my stepmom, after my mother went to prison, after I became the oldest of six instead of three.

I picked the bike I bought at Walmart with my youngest for the color. Turquoise green, my favorite. Well, at least one favorite. I bought us both helmets. We talked about riding together, about finding parks with trails, about getting up early in the summer to beat the heat. And then we pulled into our parking space, in front of our townhouse, and unwedged the bikes from the car. We walked them to the back and locked them up—a chain around the deck post—and left them there for the night. It was dark. I was tired.

I think my youngest rode the next day, or maybe the day after. When they came back inside their cheeks were pink and their eyes sparkled, and I remembered how I felt so many years ago and when they said "Mom! Come with me it's so much fun!" I smiled and hugged them and offered a snack as I said, "Tomorrow. Maybe tomorrow."

I waited until I was alone before I rolled the turquoise city bike—I'd researched by then, learned that the ten-speed I loved once upon a time was a road bike—past the neighbor's fence and out onto the side street of our suburban Kansas City town. I clicked the helmet's buckle below my chin, climbed onto the too-small seat. I let myself wobble to the edge of the side street and back, unsure of my footing, of my ability to keep the machine going with the weight I carried. I wished for training wheels again, wished for the rush of wind through my hair, but there was the helmet and there were my weary legs and the wind, ever faithful, met me exactly where I was.

Bikepacking with Man's Best Friend
by Jim Andera

Bikepacking defined: The marriage of backpacking with mountain-biking.

In the 1960s, I grew up among the cornfields of Iowa, often riding bicycles on the gravel roads between my family's farm and the farms of my boyhood friends. At that point in my life, bicycling was more about transportation than it was about bicycling itself, especially when I was too young to have a driver's license. As an adult, I did some easy road-biking in a modest effort stay in shape and pushed myself a bit harder when striving to build endurance for a backpacking trip.

For as long as I can remember, camping appealed to me. As a young boy, I spent countless nights sleeping in my dad's old WWII wall-tent set up a hundred feet from our farmhouse. For a more adventurous camping excursion, I'd go down to a neighbor's pasture next to a creek and spend the night camping out with a friend. And a few times my dad and I camped in that old WWII tent pitched on an island in the middle of the Mississippi River. Thankfully, I have never outgrown my love of camping.

For the past 45-plus years that I have lived in Kansas, I have been an avid backpacker, spending time in wilderness areas of Montana, Wyoming, Colorado, and a handful of other Rocky Mountain states. Each fall I am part of a team of two to five guys who spend a week or more hiking up demanding mountain trails, savoring the ability it affords me to leave civilization behind and fish the picturesque and pristine alpine lakes. On almost all of these trips, our family dog has accompanied us, serving as a valuable member of the team. Man and dog alike carry backpacks weighing approximately a quarter of our body weight, hauling with us everything we need for a week in the

Bikepackers adopt a minimalist lifestyle while traveling, carrying little more than the basics. In many ways, this lifestyle resembles that of the early explorers and pioneers as they traveled across the plains of Kansas.

backcountry, with our fishpoles being among our most valued possessions. In the winter, one of my backpacking buddies and I venture into wilderness areas of Colorado wearing snowshoes and carrying an even heavier backpack or pulling a sled. We sleep in a small unheated tent or perhaps build an igloo out of blocks of snow. And yes, the dog always gets to go on the winter trips and sleep in the igloo with us.

I cannot explain why it took me until my mid-60s to discover bikepacking. After all, bikepacking is little more than a marriage of two activities I already enjoyed: backpacking and bicycling. As I look back, I realize that the discovery started with pack dog #4 in my life; he is the one that got me involved in mountain biking.

At any one time, we have only one dog in our family, some form of a mixed breed, generally weighing between 75 and 100 pounds. Over the years, I watched dogs #1 (Buster), #2 (Tobie) and #3 (Buddy) gain excessive weight as they got older. (I, too, was realizing some middle-age spread.) So, when dog #4 (Trooper) was four years old, I decided to put him on a fitness program. That fitness program took on the form of mountain biking.

It worked like magic. Lightly-used parks and the backroads of Kansas proved to be ideal for mountain bike riding with Trooper, letting him run off-leash much of the time. Master and dog alike discovered the joy of riding/running together and staying fit together. Even when Trooper was in his final months of life, just before he was diagnosed as being terminal with prostate cancer, he loved to run beside me and try to race ahead of me with his floppy ears flapping in the breeze.

We also discovered that we could get a little taste of "leaving civilization behind" without having to travel to the Rocky Mountains. The ruggedly-built mountain bikes, with their wide tires and shock-absorbing front suspension, were so much better suited for travel on the less developed roads or trails than were the road bikes I had been riding for the past thirty-five years. Bicycling was no longer just transportation or just exercise, it was becoming a true outdoor experience by itself, enriched by being able to share it with my dog. That experience further developed into traveling the rail-trails and even single-track trails, the latter trails often including numerous rocks and tree roots to ride over and gullies and streams to ride through—all exciting challenges for mountain bikers.

Finally, with dog #5 (Brody), a 100-pound shepherd mix, I discovered the allure of bikepacking. I learned that I could put pannier packs on either side of the rear wheel of my mountain bike to carry much of my food and gear, attach water bottles to every part of the frame, and travel largely self-sufficient. A tent, a sleeping mattress, and a telescopic fishpole could be strapped on the rack over the rear wheel. Add a down sleeping bag and a few clothes stuffed into a waterproof handlebar bag—Brody and I were ready to roll.

As a practical matter, the bikepacking adventure starts well before the actual trip begins. Researching and selecting camping equipment and clothing that is compact and lightweight is a very important aspect of the planning—and is part of the fun. Those of us who practice this minimalist-style of camping do not have the protection of a vehicle or camper trailer to hide inside if the weather turns foul. I have to be able to rely on my clothing, tent, and sleeping bag to keep me comfortable. Planning the routes, studying the weather forecast, and evaluating fishing opportunities also become part of the pre-trip adventure.

Bikepacking yields many of the enjoyments of backpacking in the Rockies, yet it is something I can do relatively close to home. And unlike backpacking in the wilderness, on bikepacking trips I might occasionally come across a grocery store or convenience store, making it possible to restock the food supply.

No one comes out the winner in this bikepacking experience more than six-year-old Brody. Perhaps Brody can enlighten us with his thoughts.

"Woof, woof." This is great. After years of having to carry a backpack on the Rocky Mountain trips, I finally get to go packing with my dad—and he carries all of the weight on his bicycle! I am free to sniff and to whizz and to explore as we move along these amazing dirt roads. Humans have no idea how many incredible smells are out here. Deer, raccoon, turkey, mice, quail, and once I even picked up the scent of a mountain lion. And the sounds too are so intriguing out here in the open spaces of Kansas. True, there may be no UPS or Amazon trucks on these dirt roads to bark at like there are at home, but hey—they will still be there when I get back.

Trotting behind my dad on the bicycle can be so much fun. But then, once in a while, my dad yells something crazy like, "Brody, right. Brody, right." I finally figured out that all this fanatical yelling occurs when we are going up a hill. For some silly reason my dad rides on the right side of the road and wants me to be on the right side of him as we go up a hill. Don't humans realize that sometime the best smells are on the left side of the road? Oh well, I just have to go along and humor him when he barks these silly commands. Sometimes I wish they made anti-bark collars for humans to wear.

When on backpacking trips into the Rockies, Brody's four-paw-drive gives him a distinct advantage over us two-footed humans. At end of the day, when the humans are exhausted, Brody will proudly parade around camp with a stick in his mouth trying to entice the humans to play fetch. Just the opposite may be true for bikepacking. The bicycle gives me such an advantage over him, that on bikepacking trips I do not let him wear a pack. While riding, I have to be constantly aware of how his energy level is holding up. The animal shelter we adopted him from when he was ten-months old classified him as a high-energy dog and were they ever correct! Yet, there are limits to his energy, especially his endurance as he approaches middle age. Understandably, his energy level plummets as the outdoor temperature rises, making spring and fall the most practical seasons for bikepacking with a dog.

Sometimes when I stop pedaling for a moment to let Brody catch up to me, I scan the horizon of what I envision was once a vast prairie, with rolling hills and rich native grasses. As I do so, I can only imagine the struggles encountered by the early settlers who traveled through the Kansas Territory with their livestock or those who used draft horses to pull a plow or a farm wagon. I wonder, how did they know how tired or sore or thirsty the horses were or when it was time to rest them?

On these dirt roads, ruts, rocks, washouts, loose sand, and wet spots provide a constantly-varying surface under my 29-inch bicycle tires—

with each surface providing an interesting challenge to negotiate. Dirt roads offer the benefit of a low likelihood of encountering a vehicle, and if there is a vehicle approaching it will be moving relatively slowly. As we travel, I am constantly looking and listening for vehicular traffic and get a hold of Brody before a vehicle presents a risk to us. Still,

A bikepacker's kitchen may lack many of the conveniences they are accustomed to at home, but neither Brody nor his master are complaining. To bikepackers and backpackers alike, this is life at its best.

The singletrack trails in Clinton Lake State Park provide mountain-biking enjoyment and camping opportunities close to home. Negotiating these narrow dirt trails, often heavily laden with rocks and tree roots, can be challenging—even more so with a high-energy dog attached to the side of the bicycle.

caution is in order going up hills; hence, the "Brody-right" command. If the road has the potential for faster traffic, or we are in a town or park with leash laws, a "WalkyDog" gadget attached to the seat post of my bicycle serves as a way to secure man's best friend to the bicycle, keeping him about two feet off to my side. It works surprisingly well in letting me control both the bicycle and the dog, even if he happens to jerk to the side.

One of the biggest rewards of dirt-road travel is that every revolution of the wheel potentially brings with it something new to observe. On a bicycle, I will see and hear things that I would never pick up on driving a motorized vehicle. It may be a roll of rusty barbed wire hanging on a fence post, a daisy in the ditch with perfectly formed petals, a fresh set of deer tracks crossing the road, or an obscure sign showing the name of the school district associated with that section of land, a carryover from the days of the one-room schoolhouses. It makes me wonder who built the barbed wire fence; might it have been a father-and-son activity like I remember from my boyhood days on the farm? Or was the one-room schoolhouse similar to the one my mother-in-law taught in and loved to reminisce about?

The disadvantage of traveling the dirt roads can be summed up in one short sentence: they become a muddy mess when wet. I find it remarkable how quickly the tires become totally caked-up or how quickly the gear cluster on the rear wheel becomes so clogged with mud that the chain will not move between the gears. And getting off the bicycle and pushing it (fondly referred to as "hike-a-bike" by cyclists) is not that much fun either. However, on a positive note, it makes me think about those who crossed these prairies in covered wagons during the mid to late 1800s. What I experience in wet conditions is but a tiny fraction of the hardships that the early pioneers who traveled this area had to deal with. And unlike me, they were not able to simply pick up their covered wagons and carry them to a nearby gravel road. My muddy dog is a minor concern compared to the oxen that got stuck in the mud, burdened with the task of pulling an overloaded wagon though the sticky mess.

"Hey Dad, are we almost there? Remember, I am wearing a fur coat and this 68-degee weather seems pretty warm."

Ah, he may have heard me, or maybe he just saw my tongue hanging out. He finally stopped and is getting out his water bottle and taking a sip. Now, let's see if he gets my collapsible bowl out. Oh yes, he is getting it out. Great—I can sure use a drink. I'll bet we have gone two or three miles since my last drink.

But wait, what do I smell? Sniff, sniff. Is there something in this clump of grass? Was there another dog here recently? Or was it a coyote? Well, I had better leave my mark—just to be sure. Excuse me a minute.

Oh, I forgot, I was thirsty before I had to investigate the smell. A dog always has to make his nose his first priority.

Slurp, slurp. Ah—water.

What was that? Something moved over there in the ditch. Maybe it's a grizzly bear; I had better check it out. Well, maybe it is not a bear after all, perhaps just a chipmunk, but that is still pretty exciting.

And now Dad is calling me back to the water bowl to get another drink. Does he not comprehend that I am busy hunting? I guess I had better obey him. Not sure when the next water stop will be. I think Dad wants to hit the road again before it gets any warmer.

Shortly after noon on a pleasant October day, I pedal hard up a few roller-coaster hills, feeling the burden of 40-plus pounds of camping gear on my mountain bike, only to get to coast downhill a moment later. Then, after Brody and I crest the last hill, we descend into Washington State Fishing Lake from the west. Situated in north-central Kansas, this scenic lake is only a stone's throw south of the Nebraska border and is operated by the Kansas Department of Wildlife and Parks.

As I ride across the earth embankment that divides the larger south section of the lake from the smaller north section, I feel a sense of satisfaction and accomplishment that simply would not be realized if making the same trip with a motorized vehicle. Brody and I waste little time in laying temporary claim to a picnic table beside the lake. Without delay, I break out a sandwich that I made earlier that day along with fresh fruit and some trail mix. And of course, I pull out a dog treat and give it to Brody. While munching on my sandwich, my eyes scan the lake area, appreciating its simple beauty. As I sit there, I just thank the Lord for giving me this opportunity to be here to soak up His creation.

After lunch, three casts with the fishpole show me that the water is way too shallow on this end of the lake. Maybe this is a good time to find a campsite, then explore other fishing opportunities.

In short order, I select a primitive campsite that offers a picturesque view of the lake and that also has a band of cedar trees to our south that will provide shelter from tomorrow's forecasted strong winds. After dropping the packs off the bicycle, I grab the fishpole and a pocket-sized tackle box, clip the dog's collar to the WalkyDog and ride out to explore the east side of the lake, scouting out potential fishing spots. A combination of the park's official gravel roads and some not-so-official roads provides both master and dog a bit of mountain-biking excitement and puts another mile on the odometer.

Deciding that fishing along the dam seems like a good prospect, man's best friend and I spend the next two hours working our way south along the water's edge the length of the dam. With each cast I make, Brody dances and leaps with excitement like no other dog I have ever seen, his eyes glued to the lure until it hits the water. As I retrieve the lure, he stands at anxious attention. The entertainment he provides, to some degree, offsets the nuisance he makes of himself. Yet, I have to smile, realizing that in so many ways, his excitement is simply a reflection of the excitement I feel with every cast.

Back at camp, while pumping pressure into my Coleman one-burner stove in preparation for supper, I observe Brody patiently sitting fifteen feet away from me. He is sporting his very familiar it's-time-to-feed-me look. As I pour dog food into his classy travel bowl (a plastic whipped-cream container), I am again reminded of the special bond that forms between a dog and his master. Thankfully, it is a bond that I have been fortunate enough to experience with pack dogs #1 through #5 over the past forty years.

As I watch the radiant glow of the setting sun approach the horizon across the lake, I pitch the one-man tent on the edge of my campsite's mowed area. Taking an extra moment, I carefully adjust the portion of the tent's rainfly that forms a vestibule area adjacent to the main part of the tent, an area which can serve as a wilderness doghouse. A few puffs of additional air into the self-inflating backpacker-style air mattress and freeing the down-filled sleeping bag from the confines of its tiny stuff sack, results in my bed being ready for the forecasted nighttime low of 42 degrees.

Brody elects to sleep outside his doghouse tonight, preferring the natural mattress formed by the tall grass he has formed a nest in. After spending a few minutes listening to the coyotes howling not too far off, I say a prayer of thanks for this wonderful day. As I drift off to sleep, I recognize that the satisfaction I find in bikepacking with a dog is not based on how many miles I ride in a day or how many fish I catch; rather, it is about successfully disciplining myself to slow down enough to appreciate the natural beauty of the world around me.

Hearing those coyotes just makes me want to howl with joy. This is how a dog is supposed to live—here with my master in the great outdoors.

My family tells me that I am the luckiest dog in the world. They are probably right. I have a human mom and dad who take good care of me, play ball with me, take me on family vacations and for visits into nursing homes and even into pre-school classrooms, where I am the guest of honor. Few of my other dog friends ever get to go pheasant hunting, backpacking, bicycling, kayak fishing, and cross-country skiing. Yup, I will keep this family—if they are willing to keep me.

Tomorrow I have to remember to give Dad a big wet-licky across the face to thank him for marrying together the adventures of backpacking and bicycling. Bikepacking—it's a marriage made in dog-heaven.

Forty years of backpacking in the Rockies have given the author a strong appreciation for the value of spending time in the great outdoors, often with his trusty pack dog. Recently, that appreciation for the outdoors has been expanded to include bikepacking on the plains of Kansas. Photo by Bill Sample in Colorado's Flat Tops Wilderness.

"The Bike" by Barbara Waterman-Peters

The Race
by Barbara Waterman-Peters

A big summer event in a small Kansas town is the setting for this story.

Sunny, hot, and humid, like most in the eastern part of our state, this summer day in 1976 was to prove an interesting one.

My young daughter, her dad, and I set out from Topeka that morning, a new blue and white bicycle, an important part of the day, securely stowed in the bed of our pickup. Our 75-mile trip to my husband John's hometown, and site of the planned festivities, "Bern Day," would take us along a familiar route past neat farms, fields of baled hay, and grazing cattle. I was grateful for the air conditioning, cooling us for at least this part of the sweltering morning.

Arriving at my in-laws' house, we parked and opened our truck doors to a hot wind blowing up dust from the gravel road. John retrieved the bicycle, and we headed for the excited crowd lining Main Street, Trudy skipping ahead. Music, color, and the buzz of people having fun greeted us. My daughter spotted her grandparents and ran to them, grinning from ear to ear! We mingled with friends and family, exchanging news and hugs. We enjoyed refreshments, contests, and activities despite the hot temperature.

Finally, the moment arrived. It was time for the bicycle race! My daughter strode over to where her bike was waiting and walked it quietly to the starting line. I knew her little nine-year-old heart was beating hard in anticipation, but her demeanor was calm.

The heat by this time was oppressive, waves of it distorted the street's asphalt; even the morning's hot breeze had disappeared. Trudy was surely uncomfortable in the jeans I had insisted she wear, but I had tried to keep her cool by styling her long hair into two ponytails.

Stillness fell, everyone's attention riveted on the contestants. Six youngsters, five boys and one girl, awaited their signal.

Suddenly cheers erupted as the bicyclists set off on the block-long course, pedaling furiously! The noise was deafening! Excited families rooting for their kids! In the chaos it was impossible to see the result, but the winner quickly became apparent! Our daughter had crossed the finish line first! We were proud parents, eagerly applauding along with other family members, expecting her to receive the prize within minutes—

A hush came over the crowd. Something was wrong. The judges were conferring. People were beginning to murmur, mystified. The decision: a second race. So, for no reason obvious to the spectators, the hot, sweaty, bewildered kids again guided their bicycles to the starting line.

Once they took off, it became a race between two of the competitors: a boy on a tall, ten-speed Schwinn and a girl on a short Sears "Free Spirit" bike. Evenly matched in age and weight, they pedaled with all their might, both leaning over their handlebars, her long hair flying. Each one had something to prove, he that no girl was going to beat *him* twice and she that *this* girl was going to do exactly that! And for the second time, she did.

Shaking their heads in disbelief, the judges awarded Trudy the prize, a shiny silver dollar.

My First, Last, and Only Bike
by Sally Jadlow

After WWII everything was in short supply, especially bicycles and money. Every chance I got, I'd run across the brick street and down the block in Fort Scott, Kansas, from my parents' clothing store to Montgomery Ward. I'd gaze at the beautiful girls red bike in the window. I dreamed of riding it to first grade in the fall with its plastic streamers flying in the wind from the rubber-tipped handlebars. Never mind I didn't know how to ride yet.

One Saturday afternoon Dad came home from the clothing store to tell me, "I've got a surprise for you in the car. Let's go see what it is."

My face betrayed my disappointment when Dad pulled a rusted hunk of bicycle from the trunk. The old leather seat had a big tear in it. No paint or chrome remained anywhere—only rust. Even the tires were flat.

Dad chattered like an excited chipmunk. "I know this doesn't look like much now, but just you wait till we get finished with it. I've ordered a new seat and tires."

He droned on while I fought back the tears. This was a womans adult bike. I heard him say something about, "It used to belong to the guy who delivered the *Fort Scott Tribune*. I got it for a song." That song had nothing but sour notes as far as I was concerned.

"Here. Help me lift it out of the trunk. We'll make this thing look as good as new. You'll see."

By the time we hauled that heavy hulk to the dark basement, it didn't look any better. Dad handed me a piece of sandpaper. "Let's see what we can knock off this old gem. Then we'll paint it. What color do you think?"

The word "red" couldn't get past the lump in my throat. Tears welled and I ran upstairs.

Mom stood at the stove stirring brown gravy. "What's wrong, honey?"

I sobbed. "Dad bought a rusty bike. He says we're going to fix it. It's a piece of junk."

"Oh, honey. Give him a chance. He's pretty good at fixing things. You'll see. Go wash the tears from your face. Dinner will be ready soon."

Every time I thought about the bike in the basement, my heart sunk a little lower. Each night after work, Dad disappeared downstairs. I couldn't bring myself to join him. I decided I'd walk the mile to school rather than ride that junk-heap.

After a couple of weeks, the smell of paint wafted through the house. The next day, Dad came home with a package under his arm. Later that evening, he called for me to come downstairs. As I descended my heart skipped a beat. I beheld a shiny red bike with new tires and seat. The red handlebars sported new white hand grips with red, white, and blue streamers.

Dad beamed. "Let's give 'er a whirl."

Together we hauled it out of the basement for my first wobbly attempt to balance the behemoth. It was so big I couldn't sit and touch the pedals, even though Dad lowered the seat. That seat did make a handy holding place for Dad to steady me as he ran beside until I could manage to remain upright.

Before long I had my first successful run. Dad cheered.

I laid the bike in the grass and ran to him and gave him a big hug. "Thanks, Dad. Mom said you could do this. She was right."

I rode that bike to school every day. For the first two years I had to ride standing up until my legs grew long enough to both sit on the seat and reach the pedals.

The Bucket List
By Beth Gulley

For twenty years I wrote "complete a triathlon" on bucket lists I made with my classes and goals checklists for Human Resources at the college where I teach. Yet, whenever the opportunity to actually try one presented itself, I found an excuse not to sign up. I couldn't swim well. I didn't have the right bike. I didn't have a friend to sign up with.

Fast forward to August 2014. We threw our oldest son a going away party before he traveled to Thailand as a Rotary Foreign Exchange Student. We invited people who mattered to our son, including our friend Chai Ru, to Wallace Park in Paola, Kansas, near our home.

"What are those numbers on your arms and legs?" I asked.

"Oh, these?" pointing to the three-digit number (bib number) on her arms and the two-digit numbers (her age) on her legs. "I did the WIN for KC Triathlon this morning."

"Was it hard? Do you have to swim well? How long was the bike ride?" I peppered her with questions. My friend Jane started quizzing her, too.

By the time the party ended, Chai Ru convinced Jane and me we should sign up for the 2015 event. The next morning, I realized I needed to start riding a bike and learn to put my face in the water when I swim. Unlike previous flirtations with the triathlon, though, I registered, so I couldn't back out.

That fall I took my heavy mountain bike out to the Flint Hills Trail (an old railway that had been converted to a bike path) south of Osawatomie, Kansas. I rode as hard as I could, but I never seemed to be able to keep up with my husband as he rode his lighter bike.

Sometimes I rode around Paola, taking advantage of the older neighborhoods that still had alleys between the houses. I would ride out to the cemetery and the circus house (where the Patterson Circus used to winter in the 1930s), hit the railroad tracks, and head back home.

When winter came, I rode the stationary bike at the gym. It wasn't until spring that I started to get serious about the swimming part of the triathlon, though. I didn't like to get water up my nose, so I swam without putting my head under water. This is not an efficient way to swim. My husband and son tried to help me. We played "dive for rings" in the warm pool, so they could teach me to put my face under water.

When summer finally rolled around, I knew I needed a road bike to make the triathlon experience doable. Chai Ru and her family offered to lend me one. It was a custom-made bike designed for Chai Ru's stepdaughter who was a junior champion road biker. The bike seemed made for someone with long legs and short arms (which I have). It even had red wheels, and as I would soon learn, they would make the bike easy to spot in a crowd.

Unfortunately, Chai Ru had a car accident which caused a concussion. This kept her from competing in 2015. Nevertheless, Jane and I loaded our bikes, put on our tri-suits, and drove up to Smithville Lake. There we waited in a long line for our swim starts. Since Jane is a much better swimmer than I am, she started first. In what felt like an hour later, I got in the water.

Contrary to my expectations, I didn't drown. I finished the swim course and got on the bike. The flat course and the wind pushing me forward exhilarated me. I felt fancy riding a road bike with red wheels. The ten-mile bike was done in a flash. All I had left to do was run.

About a mile into the run course, I finally saw Jane. She smiled and waved as we passed. Seeing her boosted my spirits, and I picked up speed. About an hour and twenty minutes after I started the race, I crossed the finish line.

I had done it. I could finally cross "complete a triathlon" off my bucket list. Now that I have six years' worth of WIN for KC triathlon socks in my dresser, it is hard to remember why it was so hard to sign up for the first race. All it took was a friend to believe I could do it, and another friend to try it with me, and a custom-made bicycle with red wheels.

Bike Ride

by Sheree Wingo

At my age, just turned 65, I have a fear of falling and breaking bones. But I love to ride a bike. So, when the chance came to buy an adult trike, I jumped at it. An adult trike has one wheel in front and two in back, with a big basket in the back, also. It is a lot more stable than just two wheels. Normally, brand new, they cost upward of $600! WAY out of my price range. This one I got for only $50!

Two new handlebar grips, air in the tires, a new helmet, and I'm off. No gears, just pedal power. Trust me, St. Francis, Kansas, is not flat. Takes a bit of getting used to with the two wheels in back of me. Plus, our potholes are a big problem. Trying to dodge them, not fun! My friend, Steven, has a really nice $600 Trek and is riding circles around me. We stop and talk to Margaret tooling around in her golf cart with her dog, then stop and see Ry, Karen, and Rachel. Next stop, Church. Pastor Joe has his red Harley motorcycle out front. We stop, get off, and I almost fall over! First time getting off and my legs are very wobbly.

Last stop, home. Nope, can't make it up that last hill. So, I get off and walk, sorta.

All in all, it was fun, and I will ride again.

Country Biking in Kansas
by Cynthia C. Schaker

Black, shiny, and brand new. That's my memory of the Hopalong Cassidy bike of sixty-some years ago. Living in rural Greenwood County, Kansas, our farm family couldn't afford very much that was brand new. With the name Hopalong Cassidy along the exceptionally thick crossbar, it was a cowboy bike if there was such a thing. My older brother, Roger, was first in line to ride since that's the way it worked with birth order. With its glossy black finish, it was a remarkable sight! I've seen a few costly ones on eBay, but I don't remember ours having a rifle holder with toy rifle and saddle bags mounted on the bike. It seemed extremely elegant to this country girl, but my experience with elegance was nonexistent. My grandparents may have purchased it for us since they were prone to buy us gifts we could all use. My mom told me later that they got it for Roger, my older brother, so he could learn to ride a bike. Roger wasn't interested in it at all. He preferred to borrow my mom's clothespins and line them up for battle. Not sure how old we were, but I could not wait for my turn to get on that bike. And with Roger not inclined to ride, I didn't have to wait.

I've seen those pictures of children in helmets, knee pads, and training wheels with a parent running alongside them on a smooth, flat sidewalk. But most Kansas farm kids didn't have an even surface on which to practice and learn. No smooth pavement for us. No training wheels. No soft places to land. At our farm home, we did have a graveled circle drive that sloped downward from the house and curved around to the country road. To the north was a dirt road and closer to Hamilton. The south road was graveled and used after a big rain or when headed to Eureka for groceries or grandparent visits. With Daddy feeding cattle or plowing a field and Mom weeding the garden or canning green beans, I had to develop my own plan to master Mr. Hopalong Cassidy without someone running alongside.

I had two mounting methods if I remember right. First, I started from a standstill and mounted the bike and almost immediately found my way to the graveled drive. Then I discovered that a running mount gave me time and distance to get the pedals going. The falls were a little more brutal and permanently skinned my knees, but that bike presented a challenge I was determined to master. Then one day, everything came together, and I no longer needed the running start nor the slope of the driveway. I was so excited to have taught myself to ride the bike and bragged to my older brother just to irritate him. Roger was unimpressed. He was content with his troop of clothespins and war games.

Country biking was a lonely pastime for me as I had no neighbors near enough to ride with. I had two brothers and a sister, but we only had one bike, so we couldn't ride together even as the others learned to ride old Hopalong! When I grew older and began spending the night with friends in town, I had the skill needed to ride around town with my friends. How wonderful it was to ride on paved roads rather than gravel. Since my bike wasn't in town, we'd look for one to borrow while I was visiting. Usually, we'd borrow a brother's bike and hit the streets of Hamilton. Our ride would often include a stop at Holmes Sundries, complete with its old-fashioned soda fountain, penny candy, and owner Hazel at the counter. We'd drag Main from one end to the other, a process we'd repeat four or five years later in our cars.

Upon entering my teens, a friend began holding slumber parties for our group. One of our favorite adventures involved sneaking out in the middle of the night and riding the streets of Hamilton. We felt a special kind of freedom on those after-midnight rides in our small town. It was safe and harmless fun, but since we snuck out of the house, we felt brave and courageous.

Biking presented more adventures in college and beyond, but the bike which remains in my heart is the shiny black Hopalong Cassidy bike of the 1950s in Greenwood County, Kansas. That special bike gave me my start on two wheels.

Bicycles: Bane or Boon
by Brenda White

My relationship with bicycles has always been problematic. Learning to ride was a torturous, fear-inducing experience for my uncoordinated self, and it took a few wrecks and gravel in my knees, Dad yelling in my ears to keep the pedals moving. Yet once I figured out the balance and motion, bike riding was exhilarating. Along with gaining balance, I had to let go of fear of movement or moving fast to learn to ride. Once I did learn, a bicycle became a means of transportation and of freedom in incremental degrees.

First, my sister and I were allowed to ride in the yard, and then only on the graveled streets in our neighborhood and not the more trafficked asphalt pavement in front of our house. We rode two old bicycles; one actually was my mother's childhood bike and the other bike was smaller, but just as old. We rode on the gravel to our friends' houses to play, or to our great aunt's house only a short "L" shape away for a quick visit, or just rode the bikes to feel the wind on our faces and in our hair. We put a lot of dusty miles on those old bicycles.

Then after a time, Mom and Dad bought us brand new bicycles, hot pink with banana seats, sissy bars, and pink, glittery handgrips. For a while the gravel-only rule still applied, but eventually Mom gave in, and we glided on the pavement in bicycle heaven. Always careful with the traffic, we didn't want to lose our asphalt privileges, but we began to venture farther away from the neighborhood.

Our biggest adventure became riding up Old 50, as the highway was called, all the way to the river bridge and then the long trip back home. These were always summer treks as we never rode that far during the school year. So we managed the two to three mile distance and thought we had cut a real adventure duster. Mostly, I remember the endless pedaling, the heat, and thinking we would never reach the river bridge. There was little traffic, and we felt like we were the only ones on the old highway. Most trips were long and uneventful, but two stand out in memory like technicolor clips spliced into an old black-and-white movie.

In the first memory, we rode our route to the river bridge and turned around heading for home, as usual. We hadn't traveled far when we came to an empty field we had passed before. Out of the line of trees on the field's north end, suddenly a white-tailed buck jumped out and stopped to stare at us. I don't remember how long he stood there. I just remember the dark green of the treeline and brush behind him, the golden light from an afternoon sun, and his red-brown fur and his antlers. He wasn't that far away from us, and time seemed to stop as we gazed at the stag and he continued to stare back. Then as quickly as he appeared, the buck whirled back in the direction he came from and disappeared in the greenery. It was as if he had never been there, but he had, and my sister and I both got to see him. This was a spectacular event for us.

The second memorable trip up Old 50 was yet another summertime trek to the river bridge. When we started out, the sky was clear, the sun out. It was hot and incredibly humid, which should have been a sign of what was coming, considering Kansas weather. We were two-thirds of the way back home when a wall of clouds came in from the northwest. They were black, not grey or dark blue, and moving rapidly toward us. In no time at all, the storm was upon us with blustery wind, a darkened sky, and the beginning spatter of raindrops. Then the rain began in earnest. We were pelted with cold drops, and just as I was wondering how we would make it home in this mess, a familiar blue Chevy pickup rambled up to our rescue. Mom and Dad had seen the fast-moving storm and sped up Old 50 to retrieve us and our bicycles in the storm. We rode in the truck bed, completely soaked, but thankful our trip home would be swift. All I remember from that point on was the relief I felt in our rescue, but that was years ago.

It's been some time since I've been on a bicycle, twenty years or so. Everyone says you never forget how to ride, but I'm reluctant to prove them right or wrong. I'm too old to find I have lost my balance on a bicycle.

In talking with a friend, we decided driving cars ended most of our bicycle travel, trading two tires in for four with less exertion and more comfort. I don't miss the pedaling, but there is something about riding a bicycle, the closeness to the scenery and open feel of the road that you don't get from driving a car. We still see deer in fields along the roads and highways, but those sightings hardly compare to seeing that buck jump out from a treeline. Still, riding in the rain and lightning in a car beats bicycling through a thunderstorm any time. My relationship with bicycles is not a love/hate proposition, but even after all these years, I guess it is still a bit problematic.

Russell Specialty Books and Gifts

New Location—626 N Main Street, Russell, Kansas • 785-445-8353

General interest bookstore highlighting Kansas authors and Kansas history plus large selection of children's books.

Linda Crowder, owner, is a mystery writer,
career coach, and coaches independent authors.

Going to C'ago
by Carolyn Hall

My son, Clay, inherited a bright red, three-wheeled trike from his older sister when he was three years old. He rode his foot-powered trike at high speed wherever he went. That toy traveled many miles, not only from Clay's adventures but from all our family's relocations. My husband's job took us from Kansas to Missouri, then Germany, and finally back home to Kansas in a few short years.

When Clay mounted his wheels, he wasted no time. His little feet worked that trike to its limits.

I'm not sure when or why, but one day, when he whizzed by me, I asked him, "Where you do you think you're going in such a hurry, Chicago?"

He nodded and said, "Going to C'ago." After that, no matter where we lived, Clay always headed to C'ago on his daily rides until he outgrew the trike.

Life took Clay many places. His college career started at KU with the intent to go to medical school, then an outdoor leadership semester in Baja California, a brief stint at K-State, and a return to KU ending with an engineering degree.

He worked as an engineer in Missouri and then Colorado for a few years until his desire to become a doctor reignited. Clay returned to Kansas and attended the University of Kansas Medical Center.

Medical students apply for residencies in their fourth year. In March of that year, they list their top five choices in preparation for what's called Match Day. On that day in March, medical students from all over the United States open sealed envelopes to find out their fate. A complex computer system known as the National Resident Matching Program sorts through about 34,000 medical students and nearly 30,000 residency spots to find their matches.

This day is intense. Parents and friends gather to watch their soon-to-be doctors open their envelopes and reveal their destinations. For some, it's a dream come true, and for others that didn't get the match they hoped for, it can be a disappointment.

We watched as Clay got called on stage and handed his envelope. I held my breath as he opened it. He looked up with a big grin and announced, "Emergency Medicine, University of Chicago Medical Center." His first choice.

Clapping and cheers went up in the auditorium.

After a family celebration, I reverted to my teenage years. I got a white window marker and wrote a message on Clay's car windows. "Going to C'ago."

When Clay's friends asked him what that meant, he explained, "Mom did that. She says I've been heading to Chicago since I was three years old."

Bikes

by Mike Marks

My first bicycle came from Sears, Roebuck & Company, and it was no ordinary two-wheeler. Actually, it had four wheels—training wheels. The J. C. Higgins model—I called it Higgins—had a cowboy motif: a toy shotgun on the rail, a saddle seat, and saddlebags fringed like horses' manes. J. C. was a real guy (with no middle name) who worked at Sears in the early twentieth century. Sears borrowed his name to label its sporting goods, recreational equipment, and firearms.

Higgins was my first vehicle of independence. Soon the training wheels were off, and so was I. I could ride him anywhere, any time; nobody cared.

As I grew, I got bigger bikes, always with saddlebags to hold my stuff, like tennis racquets, baseball gloves, or fishing rods. I dug my own worms and rode to a secret pond across town to tempt carp and catfish. On a good day, one saddlebag was filled with catfish. Even after the long bike ride home, they would reawaken in the kitchen sink as I prepared to clean them.

Steve, a guy my age, bragged about trapping animals for their pelts. I had to try it. I went to the only sporting goods store in town—the place I got my golf, tennis, baseball, and fishing gear—and picked out a couple of spring traps. Following Steve's directions, I went into the woods where Steve said he was successful, nailed the traps to tree bases, and baited them with bacon. One trap was gone the next day when I checked; the other was untouched.

Steve told me a big possum must have got caught and yanked the trap loose. I knew Steve was lying. He confessed and gave me back my trap. Next time, I trapped in a woodland across town near my secret fishing hole.

I rode my bike back there the following morning with a hammer and baseball bat in one saddlebag. The first trap was empty, but the bacon was gone. Deeper in the woods, a raccoon was placidly sitting where my other trap was placed. The animal looked tame like a housecat with one rear leg firmly secured in the jaws of my spring trap.

I wish I could have freed my catch, but I was more afraid of it than it of me. With only a hammer (to remove the trap from the tree) and a baseball bat, I was afraid to get close enough to use my hammer. I undertook the unenviable task of ending the defenseless animal's life. It felt like forever, clubbing it with my bat. The creature winced as I struck it. It never cowered or whimpered. It just watched me with sad eyes as I pounded it over and over. When I was fairly certain it was dead, I put him, trap and all, into my empty saddlebag and rode him home.

I didn't want to ask Steve how to properly skin the raccoon for its hide. I called my little buddy, Bubbles, instead. We called him Bubbles because he had a round face on top of a roundish torso. He didn't get good grades, but he was fearless around gory stuff.

But this was sixth grade, and we had dancing school that night. Bubbles came over with his black hair slicked back, impeccably dressed in a suit and tie over a starched white shirt. He removed his coat and tie, rolled up his sleeves, and went to work with a razor blade skinning the raccoon more precisely than I skinned catfish. Despite his poor performance in school, he was destined to become a surgeon.

After Bubbles removed the hide, a virtually bloodless procedure, the remains still looked like an animal, an animal that I had killed. Then Bubbles eagerly proceeded to open the remains so he could peruse its innards. He stapled the pelt to a plywood board, and we were done. We got cleaned up and went to dance class, two clumsy fellows not quite comfortable yet leading young ladies in waltz-step.

Soon the raccoon pelt attracted maggots and made it to the garbage can before it was tanned. I traded my traps with Steve for a hockey stick.

In high school, my friend Harvey gave me a great deal on his starter bike, a 125CC Ducati, a motorbike, not a bicycle. He traded up to a 650CC BSA. Harvey was an only child. His dad was a downtown lawyer. Harvey could get anything he wanted.

In February 1966, my brother Larry emptied the Ducati's gas tank and shipped it to Kansas via Railway Express. I picked it up at the Manhattan train station, wheeled it to a gas station, and all of a sudden, I was a freshman at Kansas State University with coveted transportation.

I drove fellow dormmates over the hill to the Holiday Inn for coffee, sometimes carrying as many as three passengers, even though it was the smallest of motorcycles. Just for kicks, we had eight on it once, motoring across the dorm parking lot. I never owned a helmet.

I had three roommates in my economical dorm. One was a bible thumper with grimy glasses. Another was a dumbass fresh off the farm. I didn't hang out with either of them. The third, Rich, was a smug son of a buck from Detroit. He thought all Kansans were hayseeds. He had a superiority complex about him, but tolerated me, because I was from Chicago. I wondered why he didn't select a Michigan college. Rich and I took turns driving my Ducati a few hours north to Lincoln, Nebraska, to a Bob Dylan performance.

One day, I agreed to loan him the bike for a special date. He didn't ask—he just took—my favorite light blue pants to wear for the occasion. The trousers came back okay, but the Ducati was mashed. The headlight assembly was $45 to replace.

At the time, I was playing gin rummy with Howard down the hall. Our game had been going on for weeks, at a penny a point. Howard was a skinny Hungarian refugee from Brooklyn. He was fifty dollars ahead—now I'm sure he was cheating. I've always been good at arithmetic. In fact, I was majoring in math at the time. I thought I could become a successful gambler. I never accused him, but there's only one way that guy could get 5,000 points up on me.

Well, the arrogant Rich talked Howard into transferring the debt from me to him. I never found out what Howard got out of the deal, but I was stuck with paying for Rich's damage.

I got the Ducati back together and made a lot more trips with other friends over the hill to the Holiday Inn for coffee, until the motorbike blew up toward the end of the year. Rich went back to Michigan and never came back. I changed my major to chemical engineering.

Tour de Kansas

by Harland Schuster

Once you learn how to ride a bike, you never forget. But modern technology has improved the noble invention by marrying a motor and battery to a conventional bicycle frame. The strange love child resulting from this unlikely marriage is called an electric bike, or "e-bike" for short. You still have to pedal and shift gears, but the motor provides varying assistance depending on the level you select—as long as the battery holds out. The result is a much more enjoyable riding experience for folks like me who don't ride a bike regularly and who realistically wouldn't otherwise put forth the effort needed to explore the growing network of bike trails in the Sunflower State.

Suzanne and I had ridden our e-bikes on some shorter trails, but by Labor Day weekend of 2021, the time seemed right to conquer the Mother of All Kansas Trails—otherwise known as the Flint Hills Trail, easily the longest in the state. Under the rails-to-trails program, this former Missouri Pacific railroad route, abandoned since the merger of the Missouri Pacific and Union Pacific in the 1980s, is being converted into a walking and biking path. Currently open for hiking and biking from Osawatomie to Council Grove, it spans a distance of more than 100 miles, but will eventually go west beyond Council Grove and all the way to Herington.

The most sensible first step for tackling a trail this long should call for serious planning, but we skipped most of this step, instead opting for the more flexible approach of flying by the seat of our pants. We scored a house located just off the trail in Ottawa via Airbnb. Using this as a base camp for the next couple days, we would drive west to Council Grove first thing each morning to unload the bikes, riding the trail from west to east. Suzanne would ride along for as far as she wanted, then bike back to the trailhead and provide support when she wasn't checking out antique stores along the route. My goal for the first day was to pedal all the way from Council Grove to Ottawa, leaving the remaining twenty or so miles from Ottawa to Osawatomie for the next day.

A knot formed in my stomach as we unloaded the bikes at the Council Grove trail head. I recognized the feeling. It was the same feeling I'd had on the school bus while on my way to my first day of Mrs. Grimm's Kindergarten class. It recurred when I'd signed my first mortgage. It was just starting to occur to me how crazy an idea it really was to think I could bike all the way from Council Grove to Ottawa in a day. Good grief, it had just taken us an hour and a half to drive the distance at highway speed. Google Maps shows you can bike the trail from Council Grove to Ottawa in five hours and forty-six minutes. Sure, Lance Armstrong could do it in that time, but I'd been led down the Google Maps garden path too many times to accept its time estimate as fact.

From Council Grove, the trail first heads south by southeast, initially lined with trees, but soon enough it breaks out into open farming country. Soon we pedal past Allegawaho Memorial Heritage Park. Owned and maintained by the Kaw Tribe, which was forcibly moved from Kansas to Oklahoma in 1872, this 168-acre site is about all that remains to remind us of the people for which the state of Kansas is named.

Continuing through open farm country, we turn straight east, then head north by northeast just after crossing the fairly impressive bridge over Rock Creek. Judging from the height of the bridge, and from the size of the flood debris, I suspect the sluggish stream we cross on this day might have a fiercer demeanor in times of flood. Looking north from the bridge I can see evidence of flooding earlier this year. It looks like about a quarter of the corn crop has been wiped away, illustrating the dilemma of farming a creek bottom: The force which in some years vexes the land is the same force by which the bottomland's rich soil is sweetened. Something similar plays out in our own lives, in both small and large ways.

The trail is climbing now, departing the farm fields as it starts to thread itself through the hills of emerald late summer tallgrass. These are the Flint Hills for which the trail is named. Then the trail briefly rubs shoulders once more with a patch of trees, this time along Bluff creek, a tributary of Rock Creek. There is no obvious evidence visible from the trail, but the town of Comiskey once existed here. A small cemetery about a mile north is all that remains of the dreams, sweat, and toil that were put forth here to form the settlement. Just like pulling your hand out of a bucket full of water, man's efforts put forth on this spot to tame nature have vanished without leaving any sign.

Uphill and into the wind we continue. We have crossed from Morris into Lyon County, and on the horizon to the south, three horsemen work a lone cow through a huge pasture towards a corral and waiting cattle trailer. Evidently this lone critter had slipped an earlier dragnet which swept her herd from the pasture. All over the grasslands, cowboys are removing their stock from summer pasture. The cowboys aren't the only ones preparing for the coming winter. Every now and then we pass through swarms of dragonflies heading south. The restless wind from that direction appears to momentarily hold them motionless, but an instinct we can't comprehend drives the insects to relentlessly head south and away from the coming killing frost. Monarch butterflies, too, occasionally glide southward, finding shelter from the stronger gusts inside the manmade limestone canyons through which the trail has been occasionally passing since Bluff Creek. How do these insects know winter is coming and how does this trigger them to migrate a thousand miles or more to a place they've never been? I've been known to become lost and disoriented in a parking lot, yet these creatures, on wings appearing much too delicate for the task, have been making this annual journey for eons.

Making our way in a mostly eastwardly direction, and continuing to climb uphill, the trail crosses a gravel road. It has been miles since we've crossed a road, so it almost comes as a surprise. Two miles to the north of the intersection is an abandoned Atlas missile base built in the late 1950s. Designed to withstand a nuclear strike near-miss, the concrete shelter remains largely unchanged even though active service at the site only lasted a couple years. The threat of a nuclear war with the Soviet Union in those early days of the Cold War seemed so imminent that the hastily developed Atlas rockets were pressed into active military service even though twenty-five percent of their test launches ended as fireballs on the launch pad. But they were the best deterrent available at the time, so while the longer range and more reliable Titan and Minute Man missiles were being developed, the Atlas was thrown into the breach as a stop-gap measure. Soon the Air Force was bolting atomic warheads onto the Atlas missiles, placing them in cement protective structures, spacing them far apart in the Kansas countryside, hoping the Russians couldn't take them all out at once in a Pearl Harbor style sneak attack. Nearby grazing cattle didn't give the gleaming stainless steel doomsday missiles much thought, but the sight did give the local cow punchers and clod kickers something to ponder as the bases appeared across the Kansas prairielands with the speed of chicken pox popping up on a preschooler's forehead.

Just a bit further along, we come upon Bushong, named for Albert "Doc" Bushong, practicing dentist, professional baseball player, and inventor of the baseball catcher's mitt. Even being named for an important historical sports figure hasn't been enough to save the town. The relentless economic forces which have wiped every trace of Comiskey from the landscape are hard at work here, too. We leave the trail briefly to tour what is left, riding up a street towards what appears to be the remnants of the town's school poking up through an overgrown canopy of trees. About a block south of the school, a car door opens as I pedal past. "Hello," I shout, greeting the man as he emerges. He eyes me suspiciously but otherwise doesn't acknowledge me. The late morning sunlight glares off his pallid and flaccid skin. In countenance and physique, he's a dead ringer for the Pillsbury Doughboy. I pedal on towards the overgrown, collapsed school to take a few quick snapshots with my phone. Suzanne arrives a minute or so later and points back down the street. The Dough Man of Bushong is now in the middle of the street and is glaring suspiciously in my direction. I'm a middle-aged guy with a farmer's tan wearing shorts, standing astride a bike standing on a public street taking pictures of an abandoned and overgrown school, yet in his mind I'm perceived as some sort of threat. This is bizarre. There is no need to further raise his heart rate, so we depart, heading downhill on Main Street. We approach the North Lyon County Veterans Memorial which honors area veterans dating all the way back to one who amazingly served in the War of 1812. We continue down Main Street and back towards the trail. The empty limestone shell of what was once the town's bank is all that remains standing until we pass what must have been the town's blacksmith shop in the next block. It is a large stone building, remarkable in this town in that it has been kept in good repair and the grass is actually mowed. Other than the "Blacksmith" sign hanging above the locked door, and the "No Trespassing" signs posted every five feet, there is no further information on the building and nobody around to ask.

Back at the trail, Suzanne decides to ride back to the trail head at Council Grove while I head on down the trail with plans to meet in Osage City for lunch. The uphill climb has leveled off at Bushong, and the country, though still mostly pasture, has flattened out. Soon I enter the town of Allen and leave the trail for a quick tour of the town. Like Bushong, Allen appears to be struggling though it is not quite as far along on the path to oblivion. A young lady in overalls climbs out of a pickup and disappears into Allen Meat Processing, apparently the local butcher shop. I pass a small auto garage with two men discussing, well actually yelling, something about politics. I pull a "U Turn" in front of the stone building which houses the City Office, a faded handwritten "Help Wanted" sign in the window. On my way back down the street and before I get back on the trail, I pass a small well-kept house. I notice an older man dressed in bright red pants as he putters around in his yard before heading back into his house. Allen still has a pulse, but the town clearly would be in hospice care if it were a person. No one I've passed appears to have noticed me, let alone returned my wave as I pedaled by.

The trail closely parallels US-56 as it heads east now, and in just a couple miles, I'm approaching the next town, Admire. A small sign, the sort you might advertise your yard sale on, is stuck in the dirt along the trail as I enter town. "Restrooms in the City Park" it reads. This is the first greeting sign of any sort so far along the trail, so I decide to take a side trip up and see these restrooms. The park is on the grounds of the now apparently closed town school. I ride past some crabgrass-choked playground equipment, through a campground with spots for four or five campers, and come to the restrooms. Through the open door, I can see that apparently someone has been preparing for a colonoscopy. I lose any interest in further investigating this part of the town's hospitality to trail users. Before getting back on the trail, I decide to ride by the school. A sign reads "Storm Shelter" and the building is unlocked, so I check it out. A faded "Fallout Shelter" sign is attached to the bricks near the door. Through the door and down the steps, I end up in what was once the locker room. It has that smell that all old high school locker rooms have, despite this one having been vacated years ago. A row of mismatched chairs line the cement wall. This is the space that serves as the town's public storm shelter. In the heat of the Cold War, if the Atlas missile near Bushong and its sinister siblings had been fired, this is likely where townsfolk would have sought refuge. The official plan called for the occupants of these public shelters to munch on government-provided graham crackers and sip canned water for as long as two weeks while the radiation outside decayed to acceptable levels. Most likely, the occupants would have been vaporized as the incoming Russian missiles tried to find their mark in the cow pasture ten miles west of here. From our modern perspective, it's hard to view the Civil Defense shelter system as much more than a cynical attempt to calm public fears as we faced down the Russians while teetering on the brink of nuclear war. President Eisenhower himself remarked to an aide, "If war comes, there won't be enough bulldozers to push the dead bodies off the streets," while at the same time launching a massive effort to provide public shelters like this one in cities and towns across the nation. It is a remarkable characteristic of the human mind that it is perfectly capable of holding two diametrically opposed thoughts at the same time. Such was the strange twilight of the Cold War, which we are probably luckier than we know to have survived.

I get back on the trail and pedal eastward. The country has leveled out now and is mostly farmland as I pass under the Kansas Turnpike and head towards the next town, Miller. I take advantage of the straight and level trail and get the bike up to speed. I should press on but can't resist a side trip into Miller. From 1917 to 1921 the Miller Canning Company was producing as many as 36,000 cans of tomatoes per year under their "Double Circle" brand. The year 1919 turned out to be the high-water mark, and by 1921 the business was closed. There is no sign of it today. Fire seems to have been the town's recurring nemesis. Most of the business district burned in 1930. In 1956 the school burned down. The railroad depot did not burn down. It was instead obliterated by a train which derailed in 1931. The only thing keeping it from being a total loss was the discovery of a working adding machine in the debris. Luckily, the wreck occurred on a Sunday, when the depot was unmanned, and none were killed in the calamity. The railroad rebuilt the depot, only to close it in 1958 due to lack of business. The town's only remaining business, a lumberyard, burned down in 1960. Finally realizing the need for a fire department, the town formed one in 1964, but with no business district left by then, it was clearly a case of shutting the barn door after the horse had already escaped.

Beyond Miller, the trail is immediately flanked on the south by a large cattle feedlot, though it's hard to tell if this is still a going concern. The lots are full of weeds and empty of cattle. I cross under the Kansas Turnpike and leave the Flint Hills behind. Now the landscape is mostly farm fields with corn, milo, and soybeans racing towards maturity and harvest. I occasionally pass by a small pasture, but clearly crop farming is becoming more common as I head east. I had hoped to be in Osage City by noon, but that's not going to happen. A text comes through that Suzanne, too, is running behind. She hadn't realized that taking the battery off her bike would make it about twenty pounds lighter, so she had to flag down some help to load her bike with battery at the Council Grove trail head. Riding uphill and into the wind had really zapped my bike's battery. I'm down to one bar remaining by the time I reach Osage City. Then I discover something really disturbing. The trail doesn't exist through Osage City; instead, the old rail bed is overgrown with weeds and small trees. Old cars and abandoned obsolete farm equipment are parked on the trail right-of-way. "No Trespassing" signs are posted on city alleys which parallel the trail. There are no detour signs, so I pick my way along city streets and wait for Suzanne at the City Park. The Osage City Chamber of Commerce slogan is "Osage City Has It!", but their website makes no mention of the trail that cuts right through town. There is no marked detour, and the streets I use are not bike friendly, and frankly, a little dangerous due to the heavy car traffic. This is too bad since Osage City, because of where it is situated on the trail, could really cash in on trail users needing a place to eat, sleep, or just rest. They're not just killing the Goose that laid the Golden Egg; instead, they seem to be denying that there is even a Goose in the first place. Suzanne finally catches up with me and, after a late lunch, I swap out my battery for the one Suzanne had only partially used, and finally manage to find the trail again on the east edge of Osage City. We put my battery on a charger in the truck because I have a feeling the charge that's left in Suzanne's battery won't get me all the way back to Ottawa.

East of Osage City, the trail runs straight as a string heading east and paralleling the highway, K-31, less than a quarter mile to the south. Traffic noise from the highway and the generally uninspiring landscape of cropland could make this a good stretch to put the hammer down and make up time, if only the trail surface allows this. Upon entering Osage county, the trail's surface was noticeably degraded. Most of the Flint Hills Trail is paved with packed limestone chips making a great biking surface, but here the surface is mostly dirt with occasional chunks of railroad ballast stone mixed in with potholes and ruts. Luckily, it is dry for my trip because I can see this stretch being a muddy mess after a rain. After crossing over US-75, I start to get the feeling I'm in the home stretch, and I may actually pull this ride off after all.

The trail surface improves again near the town of Vassar. I take a quick detour through town even as thunderhead clouds become visible on the western horizon. There's not much reason to stop or even slow down in Vassar, so I'm back on the trail heading east, racing the setting sun and approaching storms. All that high-speed riding from Osage City has really drained the battery, so despite the spotty cell service, I manage to get a text to Suzanne to have her meet me at the Pomona trail head with the battery which has been charging since we had lunch in Osage City. The trail between Vassar and Pomona is truly beautiful in an eastern Kansas sort of way. There are bridges across creeks, and stretches of trail pass through trees forming a tunnel of leaves. About a mile west of Pomona, my battery, which has been down to one bar for a while, finally cuts out completely, so it's back to pedaling the old-fashioned way, deadheading to the Pomona trail head. As if we'd planned it that way all along, Suzanne pulls into the trailhead parking lot at exactly the same time I get there. With the sun nearing the horizon and storm clouds approaching, this bit of good timing should have been taken as a sign to stop for the day, but on the map it doesn't look too far from Pomona to Ottawa, and the battery is showing three bars. It should be more than enough to blow down the rest of the trail at high speed. So, reloaded with Gatorade and a "sort of" charged battery, I head east again on the final leg of the trail into Ottawa.

It's just a few miles to Ottawa, so I bump the assist level up and pick up speed. For a ways, the trail so closely parallels the heavily used BNSF mainline railroad that I can feel the heat and smell the diesel exhaust as the long container trains blast past on the nearby rails. Then without any warning, the trail ends abruptly. There is a barricade across the trail and trees growing where the trail should be. A faded sign points to a detour route using gravel roads. In my research, I hadn't seen anything about this detour, but clearly it has been here for quite some time. The gravel road twists and turns and passes through intersections which are usually marked with small, faded detour signs. Eventually, I make a wrong turn, and in the fading daylight head in the wrong direction. Having not seen any of the little detour signs in a while, I pull off the gravel road at a small cemetery and take a look at Google Maps. I should have done this long before now instead of relying on those sparse detour signs. Going up and down the hills on the gravel road detour has taken a serious toll on my battery, which is down to one bar. By now it is not only getting dark, but storms are close enough to cause real concern.

With no margin for error, I figure out where I made the wrong turn and head back down the road I've just traveled, all the way back to the intersection where I made my mistake. I try to nurse what little power is left in the battery by coasting down hills and setting the assist to its lowest level. I'm within sight of where the detour rejoins the trail when the battery finally throws in the towel. I have enough juice to run the headlight, but there's nothing left for pedal assist. I could give in and call Suzanne for a ride, but by now I can see the lights of Ottawa, so I figure I can just deadhead into town. Luckily, the trail is level and well maintained at this point. It's hard, but not impossible to pedal the bike after a full day on the trail. I accomplish this by gearing down and going slow. Soon the trail passes over the Marais Des Cygnes River on a grand old steel truss bridge which I can just make out in the fading twilight. I pedal on and can make out the tombstones of a large cemetery just west of the trail. Then I pass the ball fields on the north edge of town just as they're turning out the lights. From there the trail is dumped onto the edge of a city street, before finally joining the Prairie Spirit Trail which runs north to south through Ottawa. By this point I'm following the directions Google Maps generates, long since too tired to question their accuracy. As I pedal slowly through Legacy Square Park, I notice a pile of clothing near the public restroom. Then the pile of clothing moves, and I realize it's a person, a homeless person who has chosen the sidewalk in front of the public restroom as a camping spot for the night. Lightning flashes in the night sky off to the west as I finally make my way into the driveway of the house we have rented. I've been on the trail for twelve hours, and the bike's odometer reads eighty-two miles. Suzanne opens the door as I stagger inside. Apparently, I look a little rough. I inhale some food, wash off the trail dirt with a quick shower, and collapse into bed. It doesn't take long to fall asleep. It would take an explosion to wake me up, and as it turned out, there was one during the night when the storms finally arrived and lightning hit somewhere close enough to knock some décor off the wall. The rain outside was driving down so hard it looked like the house was being sprayed with a fire hose.

After spending the next morning around the house recuperating, I'm ready for more. By midmorning, the sun has emerged, and it is time to complete the rest of the trail from Ottawa east where it ends at the Osawatomie trail head.

With a full battery and a relatively short twenty miles ahead of me, I decide to bump up the bike's assist level and just enjoy the ride. I start where I left off in downtown Ottawa where the trail follows the flood control levee, before heading east and ducking under I-35 on the edge of town. For a while, it has the Marais Des Cygnes River on one shoulder and a timbered hillside on the other. This is the oldest completed part of the trail, the part that was first converted from rail bed to trail before the state took the entire trail on as a state park a few years ago. The trail surface is in good condition, and I seem to be going generally downhill through a tunnel of trees crossing occasional streams on wood-decked bridges. I am amazed at how much the landscape has changed in the less than one hundred miles where I started in the Flint Hills to where I am now in the forested eastern Kansas floodplain of the Maris Des Cygnes River.

The trail departs from the river as I pass through the town of Rantoul, the only small town between Ottawa and Osawatomie on the trail. I detour through the business district, but there's no apparent reason to pause so I resume the trail without stopping. On the edge of Rantoul, I can see a field full of parked aircraft. Though this might be a strange place for it, this is a business that has a worldwide market in selling used aircraft parts. Just past the aircraft salvage yard, the trail emerges into an open field. For the next mile, the local landowner is farming right up to, and in a few places, right through the gravel of the trail making the surface a little bumpy as my bike's tires plunge into the various furrows cut into the trail surface by the farming equipment. Beyond this large field, the trail again finds the Marais Des Cygnes River and descends into another tree tunnel with the river on one side and timbered hillside on the other. In this stretch there is a truly remarkable view where a small creek has carved a considerable cliff though the hill on its way to join the main river. I pause here to take in the scene and take a few shots with my cell phone camera. I soon discover I am not alone. Deerflies have discovered me. One of the little devils has chewed through my tee shirt, and the resulting bite is quickly raising an itchy welt on my back. These thirsty little guys somehow know to bite on my back where I can't swat them. If I do manage to land a nonlethal blow, they fall off and play dead. They're insidious creatures, really. Back on my bike, I put on a burst of speed, and soon I'm up to twenty miles an hour. After a quarter mile, I figure I've left the swarm far behind and slow down, only to find them still with me. It is only when the trail breaks out of the trees that the deerflies figure they've had enough fun with me, and apparently retreat back into the timber to await their next victim.

As the trail approaches Osawatomie, it breaks into open farm country before it closely parallels a county blacktop. I see a "Welcome to Osawatomie" sign—unless you count the restroom sign way back at Admire, this is the first welcome sign I have seen along the entire trail. Upon reaching town, the trail skirts along its southwest edge, passing under a steel arch and ending at mile zero near some ball fields and a recently constructed trail head park with restrooms and a nicely-done information kiosk. Suzanne is having some trouble locating the trail head as Google Maps insists on having her turn down a street which has been made into a dead end due to the recent construction of the trail head. The access road is so new it hasn't been marked. Suzanne stops using the Google Maps method to find her way and instead resorts to the old-fashioned method of trying every street in the area that heads south until she finds the one which leads past the ball fields and ends in the trail head parking lot. Meanwhile, a squad of high school cross-country runners approaches. Without stopping, one guy asks how far I've ridden on the trail. "All the way from Council Grove" I inform them. "Wow!" the whole group replies in astonishment as they jog past, my mud-spattered trusty steed resting nearby on its kickstand, apparently genuinely astonished that this nearly old geezer guy they see could pull off such a feat. More mental than physical, the effort was worth it, and it just goes to show that once you learn how to ride a bike, you never forget.

Photo by Scott Branine

See more of our
cover photographer's photos at
www.flickr.com/photos/scott_branine/

I Didn't Have a Bicycle, but I Had a Paper Route:
Serving Civil Papers
by Jim Potter

When I was a young teen growing up in Skokie, Illinois, I had a friend, Jim Heinsimer, who had a paper route. I was curious what it was like. One day after school, at his house, I helped him roll up the newspapers, secure each one with a rubber band, and then I accompanied him on his home deliveries. While we bicycled around the residential neighborhood we visited, and I was impressed that my friend had his long route memorized. He tossed each paper without checking a map or a customer list and occasionally got off his bike to carefully place a newspaper on a particular porch. I asked him, "How do you remember each house?" He laughed and said, "I've been doing it a long time."

I'm retired now, but during the last four years of my thirty-three-year career as a Reno County, Kansas, deputy sheriff, I served civil papers.

Every morning our unit of civil process servers divided up papers that had arrived the previous day. Those legal papers, prepared by attorneys, arrived at our office by mail and hand delivery. We rarely had a slow day unless there was a severe ice or snowstorm. The incoming documents never stopped. We were always trying to keep current on the papers because they were time sensitive, and we wanted to be proactive, expecting that at any moment we might receive an avalanche of subpoenas, writs, and orders.

Our team divided the papers by their addresses or location in the county. Once we had our personal stack, we would examine them for details and place them in the order of our intended delivery on our route. Patrol officers worked a beat; we worked a route. Most of the papers were about debt. Those could be attached to a front door without talking to anyone. Others, like divorce papers, required personal service where we handed the paper to the defendant. On a rare occasion, if someone refused to accept them, we could drop the papers at their feet and say those infamous words from police novels, "You've been served."

If the person we were looking for wasn't home, we'd tape our business card—with our office phone number—to the door.

Unlike a newspaper route, our paper route was never, ever, the same. However, it wasn't long before I started recognizing the same names and addresses. I also became better prepared for surprises, anticipating the location of lurking dogs ready to bark and bite, and dangerous dilapidated wooden porches with rotten boards and handrails.

I worked a lot of interesting cases, some dangerous, some humorous, during my four years, when I didn't have a bicycle, but I had a paper route. I refer to one episode as, "The Order and the Towel."

The Order and Writ of Execution, signed by a judge, arrived in our office on a Friday afternoon with instructions to accompany the petitioner to the respondent's address so he could retrieve his personal property. It was set for Saturday. This was highly unusual as our normal work week was Monday through Friday.

I was familiar with the address. The renter-respondent would never answer her door to accept our papers, yet the documents always disappeared by the time we arrived with our next delivery. Neighbors confirmed this routine. When the defendant's car was parked in front of the house, the woman and her boyfriend were home.

On my way home I contacted the petitioner, the respondent's estranged husband, to get some background on his wife. He assured me she would *not* cooperate, that she had changed the locks on the doors, and that she kept a loaded gun in the house.

On Saturday, I parked my marked patrol car directly in front of the house and met the petitioner. As always, while on duty, I was wearing my sheriff's uniform, with badge, handgun, police radio, body armor (so-called "bullet-proof vest"), and a small video body camera that was recording.

I decided not to knock on the door because that strategy hadn't worked in the past. Instead, the petitioner and I entered the garage with his key. It still worked.

When we eventually walked outside, his wife pounded on her kitchen window and yelled from inside the house, "Get off my property!" I responded, "I'm with the sheriff's office!" She returned a yell, but I couldn't understand what she said. I pointed toward the front of the house, started walking, replying, "I'll meet you at the front door."

This was my opportunity to get in the house, but it was also an opportunity for her to shoot me if she was so inclined. When she opened the door a few inches, I was focused to immediately observe her hands. I said, "I have a judge's order permitting your husband to pick up some listed property." As I showed her the order, I put one big foot inside the door to prevent it from closing.

It was then she swung the door wide open. She didn't have a weapon. Instead, she was holding a hot pink towel wrapped around her body!

Now, there are big women who wear little towels and little women who wear big towels. She was the latter.

She started screaming, "Get out of my house! I'm only wearing a towel!"

Since she was holding her towel, I figured handing her the order would be a bad idea. Instead, I tossed it to the floor. She told me, "If you don't let me get dressed, then this is sexual harassment!" I simply replied, "Then go get dressed." She responded, "I'm not getting dressed as long as you're in my house."

Even though the scene was chaotic, I was happy for three things: 1) she wasn't brandishing her gun, 2) her husband, the plaintiff, was a witness, and 3) my video camera was documenting the event. I understood that I might need it later if she made bogus accusations. However, I was regretting that I didn't have my customary female back-up officer with me.

The plaintiff, standing behind me, said to his estranged wife, "I only want the property on the list."

She replied that there was no clothing left in the house that belonged to their son (who was in the father's custody). Then the towel lady blamed her husband "for all of this."

I told the resident I needed to secure her firearm, and she responded: "If I wanted to shoot you, I would have already done it." Towel Lady was correct. She could have blasted me through her kitchen window or when she opened the door.

I retrieved her weapon from the kitchen table and unloaded the small semi-automatic, telling her I'd return it before I left. Then I told her again, "Go put on your clothes!"

As the plaintiff walked around the house, searching for items listed on the order, his wife kept up a chatter of threats, insults, and denials. At one point she began videotaping the event with her phone, telling us that she was going to show it to her attorney. I marveled at her dexterity. She kept filming while holding her towel. Every few minutes, like a soundtrack, I repeated, "Go put on your clothes." I knew she wouldn't comply, but I said it for the benefit of her recording and mine.

At one point she asked me, "What's so funny?" She had caught me considering how absurd we were. It was crazy. She was videotaping us, I was videotaping them, and she was wearing a hot pink towel. The plaintiff and defendant might decline marriage counseling, but I was ready for a therapy session.

Gradually, the husband collected his property, periodically taking it out to his truck. I remained a doorman, keeping one eye on Towel Lady.

Just before departure, I returned the pistol to the defendant. I placed it, unloaded, on the kitchen table. Next to it, I put a clip of bullets and a single bullet that had been in the chamber.

As I left the house, following the plaintiff, Towel Lady made a veiled threat to me. She said, "I'll be seeing you around when you're not with my husband." At the curb, the petitioner thanked me for my assistance and then remarked about his unpredictable and violence-prone wife. He said, "Since I knew she had her loaded gun in the house, and since I have a concealed carry license, I'm packin'." As he said the words, "I'm packin'," he patted his sweatshirt at the hip.

I was stunned. My god, I thought. He believed he needed a gun to protect himself from his wife! Even though he had been calm and cooperative, I now realized that during the potentially dangerous domestic dispute all three of us had had easy access to loaded weapons. Indeed, things could have gone from absurd to deadly in the drop of a towel. I didn't want to imagine the bloody gun fight that could have occurred.

As I left the area in my patrol car, I considered the couple's future. Was their impending divorce just one step in a life of bitter confrontation? Was their child going to be caught in countless chaotic cross fires? Hopefully, their son would weather the domestic drama without scars of trauma. I'd just met his parents, and I felt like I needed counseling. I wanted to escape from them, to go home, but first I needed to document the Order and Writ of Execution in case the petite lady in the hot pink towel decided to pursue a complaint against me.

At the office, I downloaded my camera and began writing the narrative: ". . . I showed her the Order. Since she was holding a towel around her, I tossed *it* to the floor."

Later, rereading my report, I shouted, "Oh, no! That's not what I meant!" I quickly corrected the sentence to read: "Since she was holding a towel around her, I tossed *the Order* to the floor."

Wheels

by Phyllis A. Ericson

He knelt on the concrete and checked the sprocket and chain. Adjusting it slightly, he knew the chain had to be snug but not too tight. Soon he would know if all the adjustments were correct. He eased into the seat and then coasted his bike down the driveway. This was his "new" old bicycle's maiden run.

Clyde had come a long way to reach this day.

Born in 1925, he was a child during the "dirty thirties" and the Great Depression. The lessons learned during those years had carried him through his entire life.

Never wanting for much, and always stretching and making the most of everything, Clyde found joy in simple things.

He had grown up on the family farm that his Danish grandparents had homesteaded in the 1870s, just north of Burns, Kansas, on the western edge of the Flint Hills.

His school was small, claiming to be the first consolidated school in Kansas. A voracious reader, by high school he would read, reread, and read again issues of *Popular Mechanics* his Uncle Pete gave him. Each month, within those pages, the diagrams showed him "how things worked," and the magazine was "written so you can understand it." This was important on the farm as temperamental equipment could demand repair at a moment's notice.

As a senior in high school, he became aware of the cute, five-foot tall, dark-haired seventh and eighth grade teacher who had come to teach with her new teacher's certificate.

WINTER RIDING

Clyde Larsen: Winter Riding, *Anderson Countian,* Garnett, Kansas, 23 Feb 1995; Kansas Historical Society, Microfilm NP 4505; used with permission.

After their marriage, Clyde operated and worked for the local Co-op gas station. He became known as a reliable mechanic. He could fix about anything, from farm trucks to school buses. With a little "tinkering," he could get any cantankerous engine humming again. In small towns, most business were operated by just a single owner, and so hours were long—eight hours a day, six days a week, with Sundays off for church and the family.

As he and his wife, Lois, started their family, they relied on their Depression era values—always pay cash and save for a rainy day; be respectful and make jokes about yourself, not others.

In good weather he would ride a bicycle or motorcycle to work, ones he had saved from the scrap heap, repaired and rebuilt.

One of the advantages kids in a family have is to live with their parents and "see" their parents "grow up." Although not apparent at the time, I saw the evolution of my father as he took on each new interest.

When I was about ten years old, Clyde developed an interest in model airplanes. Each had a little gas engine and propellers that turned. With no radio controls, they were tethered by a wire, and he and his brother Lowell spent hours on Sunday afternoons going round and round and round in the yard with a little plane buzzing at the end of the wire.

However, his curiosity grew, and he turned his attention to larger aircraft and began spending those Sunday afternoons at the El Dorado airport, getting to know other private plane pilots and "mooching" an occasional ride into the sky.

Next came two years of flying lessons and a joint purchase of a two-seater airplane with his brother Lowell. They created an airstrip on the family farm, complete with covered shelter for the plane and a windsock. And then he traded up for a four-seater plane, large enough to take his family.

There was nothing better than flying over the Flint Hills at the end of a hot summer day. Of course, those evening storms could form quickly, and more than once we had to duck back to the safety of the farm amid a quick shower or occasional hailstorm.

When his canvas-covered plane failed its annual exam, Clyde thought nothing of it. Always a practical problem solver, he simply took off the wings and towed it into one of the three bays of his garage in town. There we spent countless cold winter evenings and Sunday afternoons removing and recovering the plane, giving it a new, second life.

As time went on, he flew farther and farther, as he and Lois took their friends on small jaunts to visit museums and other places in Kansas and nearby states.

However, when Clyde failed his annual pilot's physical exam, there was no way to remove or recover the years of wear and tear. He was grounded, and he reluctantly gave up his pilot's license, but not his love of flying.

His interests turned back to simpler things . . . his motorcycle and bicycles. Now over seventy years old, living in Garnett, Kansas, he spent many summer evenings taking motorcycle rides on the country roads of Anderson County with Lois clinging to his back.

As he coasted down the driveway in his newly welded creation, his hand-built recumbent bicycle, he could feel the freedom of the ride. He was seen peddling around town and noticed by several.

Always good for a story, Dad told me, "A lady came up to me the other day and said, 'You're the man that rides that strange bicycle.'" And with a laugh he had replied, "No, I'm the strange man that rides the bicycle."

Bicycles in Kansas Yards
by Sandee Lee

Stacey's bike at her driveway entrance.

"What a cute yard decoration," I said to myself as I drove down Main Street in the small Butler County town of Benton. Since I knew the person who lived there, I decided to let her know I admired her creative use of an old bicycle. When we met over iced tea the next week, I learned much more than I expected.

Debbie possesses a unique love for bicycles. "I have an eye for bikes. When I see an unusual one, I just have to have it."

In her front yard is a flower garden rimmed in rocks which showcases a bicycle displaying her address. Debbie informed me that bicycle is a Hiawatha Apache skip-tooth bike. Did you know there is such a thing as a skip-tooth bike? Me neither. The sprocket has evenly spaced gaps where we normally expect cogs to be. This bike was manufactured before WWII. Debbie traded with a friend for it. She needed a way to camouflage a poorly repaired culvert after it was damaged by a reckless driver. The vintage bicycle diverts the eye. Since Debbie loves plants and has creative talent, she placed a container with flowers in the basket and added her house number. But that is not the only bicycle in her yard.

A vintage girls bike with flowers in its basket stands in the flowerbed at the corner of her porch. A tricycle rests by a large pot of flowers at the base of the steps on the other end of the porch. That trike is from the 1930s or '40s. She bought it at a sale.

A Schwinn tandem bike stands on the north side of the driveway in front of two large trees. A sign attached to the frame instructs visitors to "Be nice or go away." Debbie said. "A half-ton of people have stopped by and asked to buy that bike. I tell them no. I bought that bike from my neighbors Dean and Ruth Goodman at their yard sale. Dean and his son Darryl rode it decorated in green and yellow to support the school mascot, the Benton Tigers, in the Benton Day Parade one year.

"I have another bike that is from my era." Debbie walked me around the side of the house. Leaning against a tree stood a turquoise Schwinn bike whose style was popular in the 1960s. It was complete with banana seat and ape-hanger handlebars. "People said I shouldn't have painted it. I painted the tires, the whole thing. They thought I should have restored it. But I didn't want to." A ring of rocks and live-forever plants surround the tree where the bike leans.

When I asked if she had any other bikes, Debbie nodded her head. "I have four bikes in the garage that I do ride. I have a mountain bike and two beach cruisers. I have another one that is just different, which I'll probably get rid of."

I asked Debbie if any of these belonged to her as a child. She said no. She bought most of them at "junk" sales, though her love for bicycles began when she was a child. Her father bought a pickup load of bike parts at an auction and told her she could put them together if she wanted a bike. So, she did. Debbie took pieces and parts and assembled them. "Sometimes it worked and sometimes it didn't. You don't know until you try, so I learned lots of lessons. Bikes are easy to fix for the most part if you can get parts for them. Working on bikes was something to do. Kept me out of trouble. Kept my hands busy."

Debbie leaned back and looked off into the distance. "Riding bikes was the biggest source of entertainment in Benton when I was a kid because there was really not much to do. It was ride bikes or play basketball." Chasing down a country road after fire trucks, riding the ditches down by the railroad tracks, heading to a pond just outside of town, and many other adventures on rough terrain proved hard on tires.

She learned to repair them. Even though it would horrify modern parents, in those days such adventures comprised a healthy childhood. Debbie has many fond memories of her bike-riding youth.

Another Benton resident has a bike decorating his front yard. While perusing Craigslist one evening, Davis came across a vintage bicycle for sale. His wife had been pointing out bicycles used as yard art while searching for landscaping ideas online. The bike he found was a pre-WWII bike. That Hawthorne bike was manufactured by Montgomery Ward.

Davis added some visual interest to the bike. "I built a little flower box out of some old wood I had because I had seen that in pictures. I put a little sign on the side that we had bought many years ago—a Kern's bread sign, an antique thing. I put that on there just for fun. It surprised Donna. She really liked it. I don't surprise her very often."

The bike has a nice, aged appearance. Davis explained they didn't want something too good-looking. "I think the allure of them is because we all have bike stories." He then launched into why he loves bicycles.

Davis and Donna grew up in the small town of Geneseo in Rice County. He says riding bikes was just how you lived as a kid. "I started driving when I was sixteen or so. But even in high school, you rode your bike around town most of the time. That is how you knew where everybody was. In this day-and-age, you have phone calls or texts. Back then when you saw a house with about thirteen bikes laying around, you knew that's where everybody was hanging out."

A smile crossed his face. "When I was about nine, for my birthday, I got the most perfect candy-apple red stingray bike with shifting gears. Oh my! To this day when I think of candy apple red, I think of that bike."

He told about a factory-made bike sold by Otasco in Lyons which had a steering wheel. He had to have one. Before long he was riding it around the neighborhood. In his words, "That was the most ridiculously stupid thing I've ever done because you can't control it. The stability is so narrow. I wiped out on that thing. I eventually broke the steering wheel. It was kind of cool for a while because who else had a steering wheel on their bike?"

Kids' imaginations were king in the 1960s. Davis tells how they would have drag races on their bikes. At some point they decided they needed to deploy parachutes to slow them down after the finish line. They collected dry-cleaning bags and put strings on them. Those plastic bags didn't slow the bikes, but the riders felt like champion race drivers.

Noise was important to boys, so they'd attach playing cards to the spokes which created a fluttering sound when they struck the frame. Mattel marketed a bicycle noise maker which Davis said was all the rage among his friends. "The Mattel engine was battery powered. You mounted it on your bike like a little motorcycle motor. You had controls on the handlebars. It made noise like a motorcycle, and it looked cool. It was a guy thing, and a bunch of us guys had them."

Once I started looking for bicycles employed as yard art, I noticed them everywhere.

A neighbor three-fourths mile down the road decorates her drive for the seasons. I always smile at her inviting yard decorations. One day it dawned on me why I liked them so. The bicycle. It was always there even if other elements changed.

Her bike was a gift to her mother-in-law from a friend who knew she wanted a bike to put in the yard. When Stacey's mother-in-law could no longer live at home, the bike was relocated to a tree just off the county highway at the side of her drive. The bike is painted white which makes it easily visible to people driving down the blacktop, even on cloudy days. She attached a sign to the frame. It reads, "God Bless All Who Enter."

I asked Stacey if she has any decorating advice. She said, "Select a theme." Stacey loves decorating her bike for the seasons. Her favorite decorating themes are Christmas and spring.

A bicycle as yard art became a decoration for our five-year cousins' reunion. A cookout at my cousin's farm, located between Rosalia and Leon, is always an anticipated event because it showcases our rural Butler County family roots. Juli loves flowers and is constantly on the lookout for unused items in the barns which she can recycle as containers for plants. She knew her childhood bike had been languishing in the back of one barn, so she pulled it out.

Juli is very knowledgeable about plants. She completed the Kansas Extension Service Master Gardener class several years back, and so I asked her for advice. She knew plastic containers would hold rainwater and rot the roots, so she lined the saddle baskets with coco fiber. It holds the planting mixture in place but allows excess water to drain. For aesthetic appeal, Juli selected both upright and trailer plants. The saddlebags provided a narrow and deep space for roots, so she considered the root ball size. She advised to think about where you'll place the bike. If you locate it in shade, the plants must tolerate limited sunlight. Generally, she leans her bike against the arbor. For the reunion, it was propped against a post at the edge of the driveway.

Placement of the bike in the landscape should give the impression it belongs there. Juli wanted her bike to look like someone rode up and propped it against something then walked off to do a task. As a child she admitted that even though she had a kickstand, she'd normally lean her bike against a tree.

Juli grew up in Moline, a quiet town in Elk County. Her childhood in this predominately rural area in the 1960s provided ample opportunities for biking. Kids rode their bicycles everywhere in town and at all times of the day. It was possible for her to ride at night because her bike had a headlight. She fondly remembers good times riding with friends and riding to the local grocery when her mother forgot to purchase an item. Often, she rode out to her father's veterinary clinic on the east end of town. Her bike was her primary mode of transportation.

My friends Kayla and Ron enjoy adventuring on the secondary highways in southeastern Kansas. One day while on a drive through the rural areas of Woodson County, they found themselves on Main Street in Toronto. Much to their delight, they came across a parade of bikes— actually a family of mannequins decorating a yard. They laughed, stopped, and photographed the unusual bicycle display. Kayla posted the pictures on Facebook which is where I saw them. A few weeks later, my husband and I made plans to take a side trip through Toronto on our way to Missouri for the sole purpose of seeing that display.

While doing research for a novel I am writing set in 1855, we visited the Lawrence area. Two historical sites occupied our itinerary that afternoon—Black Jack Battleground and Wakarusa River Valley Heritage Museum. Because it is located between the two sites, we made a for-fun stop in Baldwin City to visit The Nook Bookstore, and I'm glad we did. It's a cute little store and Niki, the owner, is a delight. We left town going west on US-56. When we turned north to head toward Clinton Lake and the Wakarusa River Valley Heritage Museum, a wonderful surprise greeted us. A decorated bike leaned against a tree in the yard on the northwest corner of the intersection.

Now, I notice bicycles utilized for decorating everywhere. I found another one in a yard on North Main Street in Benton as I cruised through town. Last week I dined with friends in the western Butler County city of Augusta. Sugar Shane's Cafe, a delightful eatery, is located on south State Street. As the server placed my meal on the table, I looked up. What did I see? A two-seater bicycle attached to the wall above a double-wide doorway.

I think I remember seeing an old bike along the back wall of my brother's hay barn among some discarded metal junk. I wonder if he will let me have it to use as yard art to lean against my hawthorn tree shading the sandpile in my front yard.

ABOVE: Debbie poses with her skip-tooth bicycle.

TOP RIGHT: The bike Davis presented to his wife as a gift.

RIGHT: Yard art bicycles on Main Street in Toronto

Meet the Authors

Lisa Allen is from Hays, Kansas, and now calls Kansas City home. The oldest of six in a blended family, her Volga German ancestors helped found and settle the township of Catharine in the late 1800s. She wishes she'd asked for more recipes and stories before they all passed. Her work has appeared in several literary journals and anthologies, and she holds MFAs in Creative Nonfiction and Poetry, both from The Solstice Low-Residency MFA in Creative Writing Program where she was a Michael Steinberg Fellow. She has twice been nominated for a Pushcart Prize and is a co-founder, with Rebecca Connors, of the virtual creative space *The Notebooks Collective*, as well as a founding co-editor of the anthology series *Maximum Tilt*.

Jim Andera considers himself to be more of an outdoorsman than a writer. For him, writing is simply an extension of his appreciation of the outdoors and a way for him to share his experiences with others. Several of his articles have been published in amateur-radio publications, such as *QST* magazine, that capture the excitement of combining multiple outdoor activities together, including backpacking, fishing, ham radio, dogs, and snowshoeing. He strives to make his writings both informative and educational, often including technical content, a carryover from the technical writing he did as part of his career designing aircraft radios. Now retired and living in Gardner, Kansas, he and his wife like to spend quiet time at their cabin near Haddam, Kansas, where they enjoy the rural atmosphere.

Boyd Bauman grew up on a small ranch south of Bern, Kansas, with his dad the storyteller and his mom the family scribe. He has published two books of poetry: *Cleave* and *Scheherazade Plays the Chestnut Tree Café*.

After stints in New York, Colorado, Alaska, Japan, and Vietnam, Boyd now is a librarian and writer in Kansas City, inspired by his three lovely muses. Visit him at boydbauman.weebly.com.

By day, **Julie Ann Baker Brin** works for public broadcasting—not behind a microphone, but handling the red tape. So by night she prefers to use the other side of her brain for creative endeavors. Her favorite places in Kansas are where she can find her favorite people: nonprofits, art galleries, and bookstores (shout-out to Crow & Co.)! She transplanted from Indiana more than half a lifetime ago and married into Park City (but refers to it as Wichita to non-Kansans; forgive her). Julie is a new-ish (and, gratefully, award-winning) member of the Kansas Authors Club and her portfolio is at juliebrin.org (and dot-com, but she's a dot-org kind of gal). Her work has been included in other Kansas publications such as RiverCityPoetry.org, and Newman University's *Archaeopteryx* and *Coelacanth*.

Growing up on the edge of the Flint Hills of Kansas, **Phyllis A. Ericson** received her master's degree in Analytical Chemistry from Emporia State University. She was the CEO of the Nebraska Community Blood Bank for twenty-five years. A 40-year genealogical researcher and family historian, she has addressed many statewide societies and groups, taught genealogy classes, and encouraged others to pursue and record their family history. Phyllis has published the book *The Larsen Family - Danish Pioneers to Marion County, Kansas 1875*, and several other books documenting her ancestry. Phyllis and her husband Ted Ericson have two daughters and five grandchildren and live in Lincoln, Nebraska. Recently they have returned to the Ericson family farm in Greenwood County, Kansas, where they spend time in their beloved Flint Hills.

Annabelle Corrick was born and raised in Topeka, lived in five other Kansas towns and three other states, returned to Topeka the last decade, and currently resides in Columbia, Missouri. She earned advanced degrees from Emporia State University and Kansas State

University and was the Kansas Authors Club 2015 Prose Writer of the Year. Her writings have appeared in *The Poet's Art, 2016 Kansas Voices Writing Contest, Well Versed,* and other publications. Her most awesome Kansas experience has been standing against the wind and viewing the vast vista of Western Kansas where her paternal grandparents pioneered.

Angel Edenburn is a lifelong Kansan, freelance screenwriter, author, poet, and semi-professional belly dancer. All of her books are "Kansas-centric" and utilize elements unique to Kansas. After growing up in Kanopolis, Kansas, in the shadow of the Fort Harker Museum, she now lives outside Council Grove in the middle of a big pasture with her fur and feathered animal "children," most of them orphans or rescues. She is self-published and published in several niche anthologies.

Monica (Osgood) Graves was raised on a farm in south Chase County where she spent most of her days with her siblings doing farm things. Often, she was on horseback, riding the prairies. Her favorite activities are reading, handwork, spending time with family and traveling the byways of Kansas. She resides in Emporia with her husband, Mike.

Beth Gulley first moved to Newton, Kansas, when she was two. Her family moved to Latin America, but Beth returned to the Olathe area for college, where she met her husband. They moved to Paola, Kansas, to raise their family. Beth has advanced degrees from University of Missouri-Kansas City and the University of Kansas. She teaches writing at Johnson County Community College. Her recent writing is included in the *Bards Against Hunger Anthology, Thorny Locust,* and *365 Poems Volume 3.* She currently resides in Spring Hill, Kansas, which gives her easy access to Hillsdale Lake, where she enjoys trail running and fishing.

Carolyn Hall is an award-winning author who grew up on a farm outside Olmitz, Kansas. Her childhood on the farm provided wonderful memories which she shared in her book, *Prairie Meals and Memories, Living the Golden Rural.* It was named to the Kansas Sesquicentennial's

Best 150 Books list. Her stories and poems have appeared in *Chicken Soup for the Soul*, *The Christian Science Monitor*, *The Kansas City Star*, and various anthologies. She lives in Lenexa, Kansas.

Alexander Hurla is a native of Kansas, having returned to his home state after a four-year enlistment in the Marine Corps and some traveling with his wife. He currently lives in Manhattan and is a senior at Kansas State University. His favorite things about the Sunflower State are the wide-open spaces, the rolling prairie, the deep red sunsets, and, of course, the people.

Jerilynn Jones Henrikson, a retired English teacher, has always loved teaching, telling, reading, watching, and writing stories. To date, Jerilynn has published nine children's picture books, an adult memoir, and a young adult historical fiction novel. Her work reflects her sense of humor, love of words, and talent for detail. Jerilynn finds her inspiration in the rolling hills of East Central Kansas. No matter the subject of a current work, she is motivated by the people, history, and changing seasons of this place. As a student of history and language, she enjoys traveling to beautiful places. But ultimately, she finds the greatest joy in travel is coming home. www.prairiepatchwork.com

Deb Irsik was the owner of Makin' Waves Salon and retired from the beauty industry after twenty-five years. She is a Kansas girl and shares her life with her husband Mike, and children John and Emily. Deb is a member of the Kansas Authors Club and Emporia Writers Group. Deb's favorite thing about Kansas is the people. "Most people in Kansas have a strong work ethic and family values. The beautiful Flint Hills and Kansas sunsets are second to none. What's not to like?" Poetry and lyrics have always been part of her life, but she felt a call to write middle-grade Christian fiction after her daughter found it difficult to be "that God girl" in eighth grade. "It is my hope that my books will encourage young people to hold onto values and faith as they navigate their teen years." Deb's "Heroes by Design" series was completed in 2020, and she hopes to dedicate her time to creating a book of poetry and continuing to write essays, prose, and fiction. Deb can be found online: facebook.com/D.A.Irsikauthor, Twitter:@Writerwannabe1, www.dairsik.com, amazon.com/author/dairsik, https://instagram.com/debirsik/

Sally Jadlow lived her early years in Ft. Scott, Kansas, and spent most of her life within that state's borders. After marriage, she moved with her husband to Overland Park where they raised four children. She is the grandmother of fourteen and great-grandma of two. Teaching creative writing for the Kansas City Writers Group is one of her joys. She writes historical fiction, inspirational stories, devotionals, and poetry. At present, she has published thirteen books and many articles. The eastern Kansas countryside with its gently rolling hills claims Sally's most favorite area of the state. Sally's books are available at www.amazon.com/-/e/B007F5H0H4

Advice from a college roommate started **Julie Johnson** on the road to writing. "Keep a trip journal," she said as she gifted Julie a journal for her summer in Germany. Turned out to be great advice and Julie has kept trip journals for all her travels since. When email and the internet became ubiquitous, Julie started emailing her daily journal entries to friends and family back home. Her son's friend suggested that a blog was the way to go and offered to set it up for her. The blog now serves not only as a travelogue but also a place for musings about daily life in Emporia, Kansas.

Amy Deckert Kliewer has lived her entire life in Kansas. She grew up in Pawnee Rock, Kansas, and went to high school in Larned. After attending Bethel College and graduating from the University of Kansas, Amy lived and worked in the Kansas City metro area as a civil engineer. Recently retired, Amy and her husband moved to North Newton to enjoy the small town feeling and be close to family. She is enjoying exploring her Next Chapter.

Sandee Lee focuses her writing on rural Kansas and Kansas history. Sandra Taylor is a native Kansan who writes under the pen name of Sandee Lee. She has lived in southcentral Kansas all her life and is currently residing on a small acreage northwest of El Dorado with her husband and two dogs. She is passionate about the wonders Kansas has to offer—the people, the landscape, the history, the culture. Currently Sandee is writing a novel about a family who emigrates from Indiana to Kansas Territory in 1855. Keep up with her writing activities at www.sandeelee.com.

Starting in Cincinnati, still entrenched in Ohio, **Mike Marks** is the first of the baby-boomers, the middle of five children born in a six-year span, a generation apart, always fighting to be heard. He was taught writing structures and earned the license to abuse them from poet laureate Gwendolyn Brooks in Chicago. He was later awarded the first Creative Writing bachelor's degree ever offered at Kansas State University. Now, with over ninety published works, Mike makes his home in Akron, Ohio, where he is an avid K-State football fan.

Kerry Moyer is a Kansas poet and the author of three poetry collections, *Dirt Road* (2019), *Rust & Weeds* (2020), and *Turnpike Prairie* (2021), all through Kellogg Press. His work has also appeared in *Astra Magazine*, *Arterial Ink- William Allen White: A Kansas Legacy* volume 1, and in the "Spoken Sonatas" project through the Emporia State University music department. Kerry is an active member of the Emporia Writers Group and Kansas Authors Club. Moyer resides in Emporia, Kansas, with his wife Sarah and their two boys, Edward and Miles.

Brandy Nance spent her childhood in southeast Kansas, Wellington, and Wichita. She is an avid writer, explorer, and landscape photographer. Her favorite spot in Kansas is anywhere country roads lead her. She believes that every trip down a dirt road leads to unexpected adventures. Brandy also is a paranormal researcher in Kansas. She currently lives in Emporia.

Peg Nichols landed in Olathe, Kansas, by chance and stayed by choice. Peg had a nomadic childhood, but after every move her mother always got her a library card, and she readily admits that libraries played a huge role in her becoming an author. Peg has been published in newspapers from the *Upland (CA) News-Herald* to the *Sarcoxie (MO) Record* and the *Kansas City Star and Times*. Her first novel, *Sidewalk Sale Across America*, is the story of steering family businesses through the Pandemic. Sabrina Harkins tries to find a way to keep her yarn shop open, aided by her husband who is a vending machine company employee.

Jim Potter is a Kansan by blood and residency, not birth. When he was growing up in Illinois, he and his family visited relatives in "Hutch" most every summer. Living in Reno County wheat country since 1976, Jim and Alex—his sculptor wife—reside at "Sandhenge," their artistic hideaway. Potter's discipline in literary work was honed as a deputy sheriff writing multiple reports every work shift. Deadlines were real; patrol officers couldn't go home until the paperwork was completed. Potter is proud of *Under the Radar: Race at School*, a play used in workshops at schools; *Cop in the Classroom: Lessons I've Learned, Tales I've Told*, a police memoir; and *Taking Back the Bullet: Trajectories of Self-Discovery*, a novel. His next book may be titled, *Mr. and Mrs. Sheriff*. It's full of stories on the sheriffs of Reno County. Check out Potter's weekly blogs and podcasts at www.jimpotterauthor.com.

Edgy Sack writes personal essays and short pieces of memoir from her home in Kansas City, Kansas. Originally from the Chicago area, Edgy met and fell in love with her husband while pursuing a master's degree at the University of Kansas. She enjoys a bit of tennis, a short jog in the woods, a smidge of classical music, and hiking with her husband She is a mother of six and Gigi to five. Some of her pieces can be found in *Months to Years*, *Ravens Perch*, and *Drabble*.

Cynthia C. Schaker (Cindy), a retired Kansas educator of thirty-seven years, grew up on a farm outside of Hamilton, Kansas, in Greenwood County. Cindy taught grades six through eight at Towanda Grade

School and served as school counselor at Circle Middle School in Butler County. One of her favorite places in Kansas is the Flint Hills because they remind her of going home. She currently resides in El Dorado, Kansas, with her rescue dog Moxie. Cindy does volunteer work in the Gift Shop at Susan B. Allen Memorial Hospital in El Dorado. She serves as President of the SBAMH Auxiliary. She loves humorous writing and penning stories from her childhood. She recently had her humorous murder mystery play performed at Cardinal Creek Farm in Butler County.

Harland Schuster has lived his entire life in the Terrapen Creek valley, nestled deep in the glacial hills of far northeastern Kansas, near the town of Morrill, Kansas. Most of his time is devoted to making a living from these hills, with the help of his wife, Suzanne; tending beef cattle and raising corn and soybeans. His passion for photography has led him on numerous journeys away from the valley where he has captured the beauty of Kansas and beyond. His work has appeared in many publications and in the book, *8 Wonders of Kansas Guidebook.*

Anne Spry got her first writing accolades in a fifth grade *What I Did Last Summer* assignment. Two journalism degrees later, after owning her own weekly Missouri newspaper for twenty-seven years, Anne sold out and retired. Soon afterwards she launched a new writing and book publishing career. In 2018 she moved back to her Kansas birthplace near the Wakarusa River south of Topeka and soon joined the Kansas Authors Club. Spry has a small press called Personal Chapters LLC and has helped birth some thirty books for clients and even done a few of her own. Her first memoir was a collection of newspaper columns called *Letters from Home: A Newspaper Memoir.* She has co-authored other books, including a true-crime memoir, *Searching for Summer: A Solved but Unresolved Missing Persons Case* that launched in 2019. Her works in progress include a memoir of her Peace Corps service in Brazil and a masterclass on journaling through trauma set to launch in the spring of 2022.

Leon Unruh grew up in Pawnee Rock and graduated from Macksville High and the University of Kansas. He wrote and edited for the *Larned Tiller and Toiler,* the *Hays Daily News,* the *Topeka Capital-Journal,* and the *Wichita Eagle,* in addition to newspapers in Austin, Dallas, and Anchorage. He now is the editor at the Alaska Native Language Center at the University of Alaska Fairbanks. Unruh is the author of *Dog of the Afterworld,* a thriller set in central Kansas, and coauthor of *Final Destinations: A Travel Guide for Remarkable Cemeteries in Texas, New Mexico, Oklahoma, Arkansas, and Louisiana.* His website, PawneeRock.org, was honored in 2013 by the Wet/Dry Routes Chapter of the Santa Fe Trail Association.

Barbara Waterman-Peters is an artist by training and a writer by chance. Both pursuits have come together over the years in her articles about art and artists for such publications as *Topeka, Kansas,* and *New Art Examiner* magazines, in her book cover paintings for authors such as Marcia Cebulska's *Watching Men Dance,* and in her collaborations with poets, most recently, *Two Ponders: A Collaboration* with Dennis Etzel, Jr. Co-owner of Pen & Brush Press with author Glendyn Buckley, Waterman-Peters illustrated their first two children's books, *The Fish's Wishes* and *Bird* which won awards from Kansas Authors Club. She co-wrote their third book due out soon. Barbara lives in Topeka and her studio is in the NOTO Arts & Entertainment District. She spent five years living in rural Jackson County and Holton.

Brenda White is a native of Emporia, Kansas, but her heart resides on the family farm in Morris County. Her most favorite place in Kansas is the woods and creek on the farm. There she has seen snakes fishing in a puddle and found a baby western box turtle at the natural spring feeding into the creek. She has had poetry published in *Quivira* and *The Flint Hills Review.* What she loves most about living in Kansas are the beauty of the Flint Hills and the state motto, *Ad Astra per Aspera,* "to the stars through difficulties." Her first book of poetry, *Blue Collar Saint,* was published Fall 2021, by Meadowlark Press.

Mary Kate Wilcox is an aspiring author from Overland Park, Kansas. She attended Kansas State University for two years before leaving to explore. As a full-time adventurer, she moves around often but considers her home in Overland Park a base camp. She has worked in the forests of Michigan, on Konza Prairie, at an alpaca farm near Pawnee Rock, and currently at a ranch in Basalt, Colorado. As an avid birder, Mary Kate loves to explore her home state, and her favorite place is Quivira National Wildlife Refuge. Her nonfiction essay "My Birds" appeared in *34th Parallel Magazine,* and her short story "Untethered" appeared in the *Tulip Tree Review.* She also received the 2021 Overall Prose Award in the Kansas Voices Writing Contest.

Sheree Wingo was born in Hays, Kansas, and lived in LaCrosse for her first three and a half years but remembers nothing of being there. Her family moved to St. Francis, Kansas, where her dad was the only telephone man. Her family then moved away, but after forty-five years, Sheree is back to stay! She is secretary for District 7 of the Kansas Authors Club and secretary at the same church she grew up in. She is very active with many groups in town as that is what makes a small town!

105 MEADOWLARK READER

A Kansas Journal of Creative Nonfiction

Issue #3—Counties

Anderson • Barton • Bourbon • Brown • Butler • Chase
Cheyenne • Comanche • Elk • Ellis • Ellsworth • Franklin
Greenwood • Harper • Harvey • Hodgeman • Jewell • Johnson
Kingman • Lincoln • Lyon • Marion • Miami • Mitchell • Morris
Nemaha • Osage • Reno • Rice • Riley • Saline • Sedgwick
Shawnee • Sumner • Washington • Woodson • Wyandotte

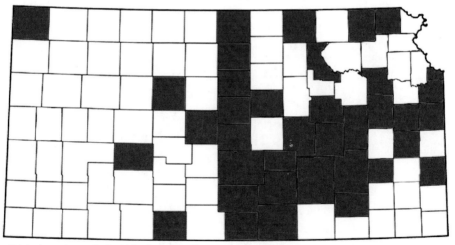

Original map image By David Benbennick - The maps use data from nationalatlas.gov, specifically coun-typ020.tar.gz on the Raw Data Download page. The maps also use state outline data from statesp020.tar.gz. Public Domain, https://commons.wikimedia.org/w/index.php?curid=570780

Lisa Allen

Angel Edenburn

Jerilynn Jones Henrikson

Jim Andera

Alexander Hurla

Boyd Bauman

Phyllis A. Ericson

Debra Irsik

Julie Ann Baker Brin

Monica Graves

Sally Jadlow

Annabelle Corrick

Beth Gulley

Carolyn Hall

Julie Johnson

Amy Deckert Kliewer

Kerry Moyer

Edgy Sack

Leon Unruh

Sandee Lee

Brandy Nance

Cynthia C. Schaker

Barbara Waterman-Peters

Peg Nichols

Harland Schuster

Brenda White

Mary Kate Wilcox

Mike Marks

Jim Potter

Anne Spry

Sheree Wingo

Books are a way to explore, connect, and discover. Reading gives us the gift of living lives and gaining experiences beyond our own. Publishing books is our way of saying—

We love these words,
we want to play a role in preserving them,
and we want to help share them with the world.

Directory of Resources for Kansas Writers

If you would like to be listed in the next issue, please complete the form at www.105meadowlarkreader.com/p/submit-to-105s-directory.html or email info@meadowlark-books.com.

EDITORS & PROOFREADERS

Connie Rae's Comments   connieraescomments.com
I offer consultation on story development, copy-editing, and proofreading. Conservative rates promised.

Curtis Becker Books   www.curtisbeckerbooks.com
Helping authors with editing, design, and publishing needs. Scheduling jobs May-July.

Well Lit Layout, Editing & Design welllitedits.com
I work with authors, publishers, and self-publishers to bring projects to life through editing services (proofreading, copy editing, line editing, and developmental) and design (cover design, layout, formatting, and conversion).

Write to Fit   hazelhart.com
As an editor and writing coach, I work with writers to help them perfect their prose while preserving their unique author voice. Please see the "Hire me" page on my website for details.

COACHING & CONSULTING

Caryn Mirriam-Goldberg Coaching & Consulting
1357 N. 1000 Rd., Lawrence, KS 66046
carynmirriamgoldberg.com
Coaching and consulting on writing, right livelihood (making a living from what you love), workshop and meeting facilitation, and creativity.

Crowder Consulting   linda@russellbookstore.com
Linda Crowder   785-445-8353
As a published author, I offer coaching for authors who need guidance
and accountability in the business of writing and publishing their own
books. My coaching focuses on the mechanics of working writing time
into your life, developing the discipline to write regularly and, once the
draft is done, how to publish and market your work. I am happy to refer
you to developmental editors, copy editors and proofreaders to hone
your craft.

DESIGN SERVICES

Author's Voice - McPherson   www.authorsvoicepublishing.com
From meticulous editing, to custom design of cover and interior, layout
and typesetting, and preparation of files for print or e-book, we guide
you through the publishing process. We also offer illustration for
children's books.

Integrita Productions - Hutchinson
www.facebook.com/IntegritaProductions
Book Midwife ~ I can assist you through the self-publishing book
process. Whether you need formatting and cover design, or simply a
better understanding of printing options available, I would love to help
you birth your book.

Well Lit Layout, Editing & Design welllitedits.com
I work with authors, publishers, and self-publishers alike to bring
projects to life through editing services (proofreading, copy editing, line
editing, and developmental) and design (cover design, layout,
formatting, and conversion).

PRINTING

Mennonite Press Inc   www.betterselfpublishing.com
JudyE@MennonitePress.com   www.MennonitePress.com
800-536-4686
532 N. Oliver Road, Newton, Kansas 67114
Printing and binding, cover design, page layout, copy editing, book
registration, consultation, e-book conversion, warehousing & delivery.

POD Print   podprint.com
2012 E Northern St., Wichita, KS 67216
800-767-6066

PUBLISHERS

Anamcara Press   anamcara-press.com
Born on the banks of the Kansas River in historic Lawrence, Kansas, Anamcara Press publishes select works of poetry, fiction, and non-fiction, and brings writers and artists together in collaborative books and projects. We are especially proud of our non-profit projects that serve community and children's art education.

Blue Cedar Press   www.bluecedarpress.com
Blue Cedar Press is "a quality small press presenting excellent and courageous literature from the depths of human imagination and experience." It proudly publishes voices from the prairie and the planet. Our books include poetry by Roy Beckemeyer, George Franklin, Kelly Johnston, Michael Poage, Diane Wahto and a forthcoming book by Julie Sellers. We also publish novels by Gretchen Eick and other prose, including Mark E. McCormick's *Some Were Paupers, Some Were Kings: Dispatches from Kansas*, selected as the Campus Read for Wichita State University in 2020-21. We published an anthology including 36 authors' writings on death, grief, and recovery in 2020, *The Death Project*, and a bilingual book about a child's experience of war, Jasmin Hodzic's *Telegrams to Angel Palmeras* (in Bosnian and English).

Kellogg Press   www.kelloggpress.com
Small Independent Press located in Topeka, KS; Publishing Independent Voices Since 2018. Open Reading Period: May-July

Meadowlark Press   www.meadowlark-books.com
Publisher of Fiction, Memoir, and Poetry since 2014. Home of The Birdy Poetry Prize.

Bob Woodley Memorial Press   woodleypress.org
Woodley Press is a small, independent press focusing on Kansas authors and Kansas subjects. We are entirely run by volunteers committed to showcasing the best in writing by Kansans and featuring Kansas. Please visit woodleypress.org for info.

JOURNALS AND PUBLICATIONS

105 Meadowlark Reader   www.105meadowlarkreader.com
A Kansas Journal of Creative Nonfiction. We publish twice each year, open for submissions May through June and November through December of each year.

Flint Hills Review
sites.google.com/g.emporia.edu/flinthillsreview/home
Flint Hills Review, Dept. of EMLJ,
Emporia State U, 1 Kellogg Circle, Emporia, KS 66801
Flint Hills Review is a national literary magazine based at Emporia State University in Emporia, Kansas.
Flint Hills Review welcomes submissions from beginning and experienced writers of poetry, short fiction, and creative nonfiction. We also feature art: full-color cover art, and non-cover art.

The staff reads Nov 1 through Mar 31 each year, and a new issue is published each summer. The magazine is 75-200 pages, perfect bound, for a circulation of 250-350. Acceptance pays one free copy of the issue in which the work appears. Contributors receive a special discount on purchases of additional copies.

Johnny America   www.johnnyamerica.com
PO Box 3 / Lawrence, KS 66044
jholley@johnnyamerica.com
Johnny America is a small 'zine of fiction, humor, and other miscellany published by the Moon Rabbit Drinking Club & Benevolence Society from Lawrence, Kansas. We post fresh fiction and humor to our web site every-other Friday, and publish a print journal about once a year.

ILLUSTRATORS AND ART PHOTOGRAPHERS

Onalee Nicklin Art   www.instagram.com/onaleenicklin
I do detailed illustration with graphite/colored pencils.

WRITING COMMUNITIES AND EDUCATIONAL GROUPS

Kansas Authors Club   www.kansasauthorsclub.org
Established in 1904, the Kansas Authors Club welcomes creative,
technical, academic, and journalistic writers. The club offers workshops
and meetings at various locations throughout the state, annual writing
contests for adults and youth, opportunities for publishing and
networking. Anyone with an interest in writing is invited. You do not
need to be a published author to join.

Kansas Book Festival   kansasbookfestival.com
Tim Bascom, Director
The Kansas Book Festival gives priority to books by Kansas authors
and books about Kansas. To apply as an author or interested agency,
see our website or email us at our gmail address. The Festival happens
in Topeka on a Saturday in September, and it includes presentations by
authors who have recently published books. The Festival also includes
booths for authors representing their own books and publishers or
literature-minded agencies. At the Kansas Book Festival, the annual
Kansas Notable Books are awarded by the State Library. We also
recognize winners of our Kansas Youth Writing Contest. Please come
join us!

Kansas Writers Association   kwawriters.org
We are a group of writers with varying levels of experience, all trying to
help each other write better. As of right now we are meeting via Zoom
at 1:30 on the third Saturday of every month. Our meetings are
designed to inform and educate with participation encouraged. In the
past and hopefully in the future, we meet in person at a Wichita library.
The non-profit group is open to any writer who wants to join. Dues are
$20 annually.

Kiesa Kay: Encouraging Courage   kiesakay.wixsite.com/courage
Kiesa Kay conducts online and in-person workshops on the Healing Art
of Writing, teaching how to transform trauma into stories, poems, and
essays that help heal the self and others. She also works one on one
with writers to help them tell the stories they most want to share.

Writer Granny's World Blog   writergrannysworld.blogspot.com
Read my Monday through Friday blog about my writing world with tips
and encouragement for writers.

Writing Contests and Awards

Birdy Poetry Prize, by Meadowlark Press
www.birdypoetryprize.com
$1,000 cash prize, publication, and 50 copies. Submit one, full-length poetry book manuscript (55-150 pages). Entry Fee: $25. Submissions open: September 1 to December 1.

Hefner Heitz Kansas Book Award   Poetry, Fiction, Nonfiction
www.washburn.edu/mabee/ksbookaward/about.html
This award is sponsored by the Center for Kansas Studies, the Thomas Fox Averill Kansas Studies Collection at Mabee Library, and the Friends of Mabee Library.

Kansas Authors Club Annual Literary Contest
www.kansasauthorsclub.org
Annual Writing Contests for Youth and Adults. Contest opens April 1 and closes June 15 each year. Adult contest is for a fee and includes cash prizes. Members receive discounted entry, but any resident of Kansas is eligible to enter. (Nonresidents must be members of KAC to enter.) There is no fee for youth contest entries.

Kansas Authors Club Book Awards
www.kansasauthorsclub.org/book-awards.html
Kansas Authors Club has five categories of book awards annually, including the J. Donald Coffin Memorial Book Award, the Nelson Poetry Book Award, Martin Kansas History Book Award, KAC Children's Book Award, and "It Looks Like a Million" Book Design Award. Authors must be members of Kansas Authors Club to submit to these awards, due by June 15 of each year.

Kansas Notable Book Awards
kslib.info/1104/How-to-Submit-a-Book
Every year up to 15 books highlighting Kansas people, places, and events are awarded a place on the Kansas Notable Books list.

Kansas Voices Writing Contest   winfieldarts.org/kansas-voices
Annual competition. Cash prizes. Adult and youth divisions. Entrants must live in Kansas. Deadline to enter: March 15 of each year.

Support a Kansas Book Store

Shop local. Support your nearest independent Kansas book store. If we've missed yours, please let us know!

Al's Old & New Books
1700 W Douglas
Wichita, KS 67203
316-264-8763
alsoldbooks.com

Bookends
123 N. Main
Hutchinson, KS 67501
www.bookendshutch.com

Books & Burrow
212 S. Broadway Street
Pittsburg, KS 66762
www.booksandburrow.com

Christian Book House
702 N 2nd St
Dodge City, KS 67801
620-227-2772
facebook.com/Dodge-City-Christian-Book-House-103903301506783/

Claflin Books
103 N. 4th St.
Manhattan, KS 66502
Phone: (785) 776-3771
www.claflinbooks.com

Claflin Books is an independently and locally owned bookstore in Manhattan, Kansas. Our inventory is hand-selected by our knowledgeable staff, not just stocked.

Crow & Co. Books
2 S Main St.
Hutchinson, KS 67501
620-500-5200
www.crowandcobooks.com

The Dusty Bookshelf - Manhattan
700 N. Manhattan Ave.
Manhattan, KS 66502
https://www.dustybookshelf.com/

The Dusty Bookshelf - Lawrence
708 Massachusetts
Lawrence, KS 66044
https://www.dustybookshelf.com/

Eighth Day Books
2838 E. Douglas
Wichita, KS 67214
316-683-9446
eighthdaybooks.com

Faith & Life Bookstore
606 N. Main St
Newton, KS 67114
316-283-2210
Faithandlifebookstore.net

Flagship Books
600 Ohio Ave
Kansas City, KS 66101
https://www.facebook.com/flagshipbooks/

Flint Hills Books
130 W. Main Street
Council Grove, KS 66846
620-767-5054
Flinthillsbooks.com

*Flint Hills Books is the only independent
bookstore in Kansas located in a restored 1887
bank building in historic Council Grove on the
Santa Fe Trail, just 20 minutes from the
Tallgrass Prairie National Preserve.*

The Nook in Baldwin City
703 Eighth St
Baldwin City, KS 66006
www.facebook.com/thebcnook/

Paper June
NOTO
927 N. Kansas Ave.
Topeka, KS 66608
paperjune.com

Rainy Day Books
2706 W 53rd St
Fairway, KS 66205
913-384-3126
rainydaybooks.com

Raven Book Store
809 Massachusetts
Lawrence, KS 66044
785-749-3300
www.ravenbookstore.com

*The Raven Book Store is a small and fiercely
independent general-interest new bookstore in the
heart of Downtown Lawrence, Kansas. Since
1987 we've served the literary appetites of
Eastern Kansas through author events, book
clubs, social media, activism, and a thoughtfully
curated selection of new books. The Raven
believes in the power of independent small
businesses to build communities and contribute to
positive change and progress.*

Reliant Bookstore
114 N. Vine
El Dorado, KS 67042
www.reliantbookstore.com

Rivendell Bookstore
212 N Broadway St
Abilene, KS 67410
785-263-9930
www.facebook.com/rivendellbookstore/

Round Table Bookstore
NOTO
826 N Kansas Ave
Topeka, KS 66608
785-329-5366
roundtablebookstore.com

Russell Specialty Books & Gifts
626 N Main Street
Russell, KS 67665
785-445-8353
russellbookstore.com

Signs of Life
722 Massachusetts St
Lawrence, KS 66044
785-830-8030
signsoflifebooks.indielite.org/

Twice Told Tales
104 S. Main Street
McPherson, KS 67460
620-718-5023
www.twicetoldtales.net

Walls of Books
733 Commercial St.
Atchison, KS 66002
913-426-6226
www.facebook/atchisonbooks/

Watermark Books & Café
316.682.1181
4701 E Douglas | Wichita, KS 67218
www.watermarkbooks.com

*Wichita's Home for Books. We are passionate
about books and the people who love them.
Complete with a delicious café.*

105 MEADOWLARK READER

A Kansas Journal of Creative Nonfiction

Dear Reader/Writer,

We are excited to introduce you to our journal, published twice each year and devoted entirely to **true stories** from our state.

If you like to read, perhaps you would also like to write a story for us. We are looking for a diversity of Kansas voices to fill our pages. Each issue features a theme which serves as a spur to get your essay started.

Visit our website for guidelines, and send us a story!

Cheryl & Tracy

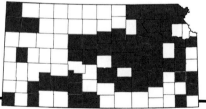

What's in a name? 105 is named for the 105 counties in the state of Kansas. In 2021, our inaugural year, we featured TRUE Kansas stories connected to 52 Kansas counties by author and/or setting of the story. We landed in all four corners of the state and then some!

Our Mission
To create a forum for sharing the work of Kansas writers.
To build and uplift the community of Kansas writers.
To share and promote resources for Kansas writers.

105 Meadowlark Reader will strive to represent the diversity of writers in Kansas.

105 Meadowlark Reader is a journal of creative nonfiction by and for writers who live or have lived in Kansas.

Each issue will contain a directory of area resources for writers. Publishers, printers, editors, book designers, cover/interior artists, bookstores, writing clubs, and anyone who provides services to writers is invited to submit details for our directory at no charge. Make sure your details are listed today. Go to:

www.105meadowlarkreader.com

Editor, Cheryl Unruh

Cheryl's sixth grade teacher, Mrs. Latas, required that her students memorize the 105 counties and county seats of Kansas. Cheryl still remembers most of them.

For eleven years, Cheryl wrote a weekly column for the *Emporia Gazette* called *Flyover People*. Her two books of essays received the Kansas Notable Book Award - *Flyover People: Life on the Ground in a Rectangular State* (2010) and *Waiting on the Sky: More Flyover People Essays* (2014), both by Quincy Press. Her poetry collection, *Walking on Water* (2017) and memoir, Gravedigger's Daughter (2021), were published by Meadowlark Press.

Publisher, Tracy Million Simmons

Tracy is the owner of Meadowlark Press. She enjoys reading and writing about the people and places of her home state of Kansas, both real and imagined.

Tracy started Meadowlark in 2014 with the publication of *Green Bike, a group novel*, with Kevin Rabas and Michael D. Graves. Since that time, Meadowlark has published books of poetry, fiction, and nonfiction, including the 2016 Kansas Notable Book, *To Leave a Shadow*, by Michael D. Graves, the 2020 Kansas Notable Book, *Headwinds*, by Edna Bell-Pearson, and the 2021 Kansas Notable Book, *All Hallows' Shadows*, by Michael D. Graves.

105 Meadowlark Reader is a real paper publication committed to including stories from every Kansas county. It is published twice each year, in May and November.

Our Reader features:

- True stories we hope will remind you of the deeply embedded Kansas roots we share.
- Funny stories. Heartfelt stories.
- Stories that may surprise you.
- Stories that may inspire you to contribute your own to future issues of *105 Meadowlark Reader.*
- Submit stories to: https://www.105meadowlarkreader.com/ p/submission-guidelines.html

Subscribe at 105MeadowlarkReader.com or mail this form with check to Meadowlark Press, PO Box 333, Emporia, KS 66801.

___1 year $29 + $4 shipping & handling + $2.81 Tax = **cost $35.81**
___2 years $56 + $4 shipping & handling + $5.10 Tax = **cost $65.10**

Start my subscription with: ☐ Issue #1 (Beginnings) May 2021
☐ Issue #2 (Road Trips) Nov 2021
☐ Issue #3 (Bicycle Stories) May 2022
☐ Issue #4 (Food Stories) Nov 2022

Name: _____

Address: _____

City: _____

State: _____   ZIP: _____

105 MEADOWLARK READER

A Kansas Journal of Creative Nonfiction

Accepting Submissions for Issue #4
May 1 - June 30, 2022

Theme: (True) Food Stories

Accepting Submissions for Issue #5
November 1 - December 31, 2022

Theme: (True) Animal Stories

Accepting Submissions for Issue #6
May 1 - June 30, 2023

Theme: (True) Kansas Landmark Stories

www.105meadowlarkreader.com